GERMAN LIGHT CRUISERS OF WORLD WAR II

OTHER TITLES IN THIS SERIES

Battleships of the Bismarck Class

Battleships of the Scharnhorst Class

Pocket Battleships of the Deutschland Class

Heavy Cruisers of the Admiral Hipper Class

GERMAN LIGHT CRUISERS OF WORLD WAR II

Emden • Königsberg • Karlsruhe
Köln • Leipzig • Nürnberg

Gerhard Koop and Klaus-Peter Schmolke

Translated from the German by Geoffrey Brooks

GREENHILL BOOKS, LONDON
NAVAL INSTITUTE PRESS, ANNAPOLIS, MARYLAND

German Light Cruisers of World War II
first published 2002 by Greenhill Books, Lionel Leventhal Limited,
Park House, 1 Russell Gardens, London NW11 9NN

Published and distributed in the United States of America by
the Naval Institute Press, 291 Wood Road, Annapolis,
Maryland 21402-5034

British Library Cataloguing in Publication Data available

Greenhill ISBN 1-85367-485-0

Library of Congress Catalog Card Number 2001096222

Naval Institute Press ISBN 1-55750-310-9

Publishing History
German Light Cruisers of World War II is translated from *Emden: Ein
Name—fünf Schiffe*, first published 1983, and *Die Leichten Kreuzer
Königsberg, Karlsruhe, Köln, Leipzig, Nürnberg*, first published 1994,
by Bernard & Graefe Verlag, Bonn

Edited and typeset by Roger Chesneau
Printed and bound in Singapore by Kyodo Printing Company

Contents

Foreword

This fifth volume of the series 'German Navy Heavy Ship Types and Classes' introduces the six light cruisers of the *Kriegsmarine—Emden, Königsberg, Karlsruhe, Köln, Leipzig* and *Nürnberg*—and is a companion to four earlier volumes featuring battleships of the *Bismarck* class and *Scharnhorst* class, the 'pocket-battleships' of the *Deutschland* class and the heavy cruisers of the *Admirral Hipper* class. It explains the development stage, provides a detailed review of important facts and figures and recounts the full service history of each of the six ships separately, supplemented by documentary references, War Diary extracts and combat reports. The text concludes with a critical epilogue. Also provided are detailed sketches, technical tables and a comprehensive selection of photographs, most of which are from private collections not previously published in this compact form and many of which appear in an English-language publication for the first time.

Without the support and assistance of helpers this book could not have been compiled. Valuable references, advice and supporting documents were provided by Public Official Galle (who placed the general plans and other documents of *Königsberg* at my disposal), and A. Didrichs and F. Bavendamm, who made copies where necessary. To all go my grateful thanks.

Unless otherwise stated, all plans and sketches were prepared by Klaus-Peter Schmolke (who served aboard *Leipzig* as No 1 Electrical Engineer Officer from 12 July 1943 until the capitulation). Photograph sources were: P. K. Koop Collection; Marine/Kriegsmarine Werft, Wilhelmshaven; Naval Command North Sea Station; Deutsche Werke, Kiel; A. Klein; Schmolke; Keystone; Dressler; the MAN Archive; the Royal Air Force; the Royal Navy; the US Navy; Spiess; former *Maschinenobermaat* Simon Collection (*Emden*); and former *Kadettenkorporal* Pogoda Collection (*Emden*).

Gerhard Koop

Introduction

On 16 April 1919 the German Admiralty was instructed to set up a 'Provisional *Reichsmarine*', this measure being legitimised by the elected *Reichstag* on 30 July 1920. The *Wehrgesetz* (Armed Forces Law) was passed on 23 March 1921. The scuttling of the High Seas Fleet at Scapa Flow on 21 June 1919 was a direct consequence of the dictated terms of the Versailles Peace Treaty. Subsequently, any new German warship had to replace a ship condemned for scrap drawn from a list of the most modern remaining after the scuttling. In fulfilment of the peace treaty, the Navy was to be hacked down to impotency. Various naval offices were closed down or merged.

The conditions of the Treaty of Versailles were harsh. The Navy was restricted to a standing force of 15,000 men and a few obsolete warships. As regards light cruisers, the *Reichsmarine* was permitted to have six. These were not to displace more than 6,000 metric tonnes, and the armament was not to exceed 15cm (5.9in) in calibre. When one of the existing six cruisers had been in service for twenty years, it could be replaced by a new vessel. A destroyer was a light cruiser if its displacement was in excess of 800 tonnes. Germany was allowed sixteen destroyers, and sixteen torpedo-boats not exceeding 200 tonnes, all of which could he replaced by new ships after fifteen years' service.

The question regarding the need for a Navy at all was considered for some time. Along with the colonies, the Versailles Treaty had deprived the Reich of various territories. Large areas had passed to France and Poland. By virtue of these losses, the province of East Prussia had been separated from the *Reich* and isolated. It seemed advisable to protect communications by sea, and for this reason Parliament was induced, with some effort, to vote for the modernisation of four old battleships, five small cruisers and a few torpedo-boats, and to recruit personnel. The latter was not easy. The confusion of the revolutionary period, naval demobilisation and the loss of many former naval men to Free Corps or other political groups made the establishment of a new permanent core problematic, and the Chiefs of the Naval Command, especially *Admiral* Raeder, worked hard to put together a selection which was later to be, in terms of human material, the firm base for the *Reichsmarine* and *Kriegsmarine*.

The *Reichsmarine* was a collection of old and obsolete ships without battle value but useful for training new personnel. The light cruisers had oil-fired steam reciprocating machinery of mixed domestic and foreign manufacture. The choice of those to be in service at any particular time was made from *Arcona*, *Medusa*, *Thetis*, *Niobe*, *Nymphe* and *Amazone* of the *Gazelle* class from the 1897–1904 period, plus *Berlin* and *Hamburg* of the *Bremen* class from 1902–04. Several were substantially rebuilt, but they nevertheless remained old ships. (Only *Medusa* and *Arcona* eventually served in the Second World War, both as floating flak batteries.) The rump of the torpedo-boats looked modern, but the largest twelve had turbines without geared drive and the remainder were mostly coal-fired. Taking an overall view of these small cruisers and torpedo-boats, it is clear that Germany had been reduced to the status of something less than a third-rate naval force. All pretensions to naval power had been swept away.

The New Ship

Soon after the reinstitution of the *Reichsmarine*, the Planning Office began deliberations for the first replacement small cruiser. This question was not without external difficulties since the Versailles Treaty forbade the construction of warships in private German yards. The major State yard, Kaiserliche Werft, Danzig, was now in a Free City which no longer formed part of the *Reich*. The yard at Kiel had been renamed Deutsche Werke, split up and partly privatised, and only a small part was continuing to function as the naval arsenal. The former Kaiserliche Werft at Wilhelmshaven was no more than a remnant of what it had once been. Moreover, hyperinflation was beginning to make itself felt.

The *Reichsmarine* applied for finance for the construction of a cruiser in the 1920 Naval Estimates, and this was eventually approved in March 1921. When the initial design work was taken in hand, a new problem came to light: the Ship Test Institute had been closed down on 1 September 1920 and the Navy had no experimental installation for model testing. This meant that recourse was had to existing Imperial Navy designs and plans abandoned at the conclusion of hostilities.

The design selected for Cruiser 'A' was scheduled 'Erzatz [Replacement] Ariadne, Office Design 1920' and was based on the plans for Karlsruhe (ii) of the former Cöln class, 'Replacement Niobe, Office Design 1914", the ship having been launched in 1916. The building contract was placed provisionally at the Wilhelmshaven yard, confirmation following on 7 April 1921, Yard Number 100. The final blueprints were not delivered until 20 February 1922 after the first keel material had been laid. This was the first large warship to be built in Germany after World War I; the design was the final Imperial Navy cruiser development updated to allow for lessons and experiences drawn subsequently; for example, in the main frame the sides at 8.96m were 20cm higher because the upper deck aft had been raised to that level.

During the construction of Cruiser 'A' the Washington Disarmament Conference took place, its purpose being to limit the naval arms race, especially with regard to capital ships and cruisers. The participants were the major victorious powers of the Great War—the United States, Britain, France, Japan and Italy. Germany was, naturally, not invited. This Conference decided amongst other things the numbers and size of future warships based on displace-

ment. The Imperial (or Long or Washington) ton, equivalent to 1,016kg, became the basis of a ship's 'standard' or 'type' displacement. This 'standard' displacement was the weight of the ship equipped to sail with all ammunition and armament and her machinery ready, plus water for the crew, in boilers and piping but excluding fuel and feedwater. The previous standard, 'designed' displacement, as understood by German naval architects, had also included approximately one-third to two-fifths of the fuel and water aboard.

The effect of the two changes—the standard displacement based on long tons instead of metric tonnes—meant that what had previously been designated a 6,000-tonne light cruiser was now a 5,280-tonne cruiser. The new Emden fell well within the Versailles Treaty limits and the planners announced changes in design accordingly, so that the eight 15cm guns would be arranged in four twin turrets on the centreline, enabling all guns to fire on the broadside; there would be four double-banked sets of torpedo

Below: Emden leavesNo III Lock Entrance, Wilhelmshaven, on 14 November 1928; at the quayside is a new torpedo-boat of the Albatros class. A recent refit has given the cruiser a short 4m pole and compass station above the mast crosstree and an after fire control with rangefinder at the foot. The guns could be directed from the foretop or in battery groups.

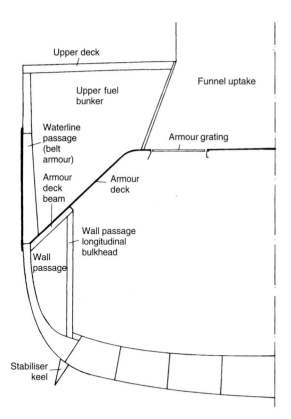

Labels on diagram:
Upper deck
Upper fuel bunker
Funnel uptake
Waterline passage (belt armour)
Armour grating
Armour deck beam
Armour deck
Wall passage longitudinal bulkhead
Wall passage
Stabiliser keel

Above: Main frame of *Emden*.

tubes on the upper deck; the boilers were to be all oil-fired; the turbines would be geared; and belt armour would be fitted.

The Allied Control Commission (NIACC) would not approve the first two design changes and the eight main guns reverted to an arrangement of single gunhouses with the result that only six could fire on the broadside. Quite apart from the objections of the NIACC, there were financial problems and shortages of material. The French occupied the Ruhr, where were to be found the main suppliers to the shipbuilding industry—and not only armoured steel but also Krupp guns. German industry elsewhere was in a desolate state, ground under by the woefully high reparations which brought in their train rising unemployment and hyperinflation leading ultimately to the edge of the abyss.

The keel was laid on 8 December 1921 and construction proceeded haltingly. There was a general lack of materials, particularly profiled steel which was essential for the inner structure of the hull. The building of a warship is always a compromise. The main characteristics requires are combat strength (hitting power plus resistance); speed;

and cruising range. All cannot be satisfied at the same time and to the same extent, and so one either gets a powerfully armed ship with a high speed, or a well-armoured ship which is much slower. However, in a cruiser, armour does not have the same priority as in a capital ship, and the problem for German ship designers was how to pack the latest advances in technology into a lightly armoured cruiser with a displacement of no more than 6,000 long tons. From today's viewpoint the solution was relatively simple. Up till that time the usual method of construction had been by riveting, and German shipbuilders experimented on *Emden* with the electrical welding process. It had been known and applied for some time previously, but never before on this scale. All main longitudinal bulkheads and the outer plating were riveted as previously, but elsewhere welding was employed wherever possible. The use of light metals in combination with welding led to weight savings of about 8–10 per cent taken over the hull as a whole. Predominantly, normal shipbuilding steel was employed, and armour was an alloy of KC (Krupp Cemented) or KNC (Krupp Non-Cemented) plates.

The hull was built to the longitudinal frame system and had seventeen watertight compartments. The frames were set 1,350mm apart. Fuel bunkers were located in the double bottom which extended over 56 per cent of the ship's length. The collision bulkhead was at frame 106. This provided the ship with a longer closed bow and assured good sea keeping qualities despite the tall command tower and higher bridge structure. Command relay, damage control and ventilation were all newly designed in the light of war experience.

In comparison to the *Karlsruhe* (ii) design, crew accommodation was greatly improved, not only by the longer foreship and superstructure but also by the space released when the numerous coal bunkers were done away with (the oil bunkers were located principally in the double bottom).

The engine room was an advance despite having four of its ten boilers coal-fired. This arrangement was followed mainly to economise on fuel costs during overseas cruises. Geared turbines, replacing the previous direct drive, gave more favourable propeller revolutions and a reduction in fuel consumption. A central longitudinal bulkhead separating the turbine rooms had been dispensed with and the modernisation of the engine room area resulted in a more compact arrangement with shorter piping. This led to a reduced armour requirement for the central hull. The relocation of the condensers below the last turbine stage reduced the dimensions of the turbine sets, with commensurate savings in engine room floor space. All these improvements were attended by substantial weight savings.

Königsberg Class

Chief Naval Architect Ebrenburg's 1924/25 design for these three ships followed the proven system of longitudinal bulkheads. Because of the displacement limit the hull was 85 per cent welded, light metal being used wherever possible. There were sixteen comprehensively subdivided watertight compartments, the hull being protected by a light waterline armour. The double bottom extended over 72 per cent of the length of the hull.

The cruisers represented a completely new type. Their size and main armament were limited by the Treaty of Versailles, but weight savings enabled nine 15cm guns to be mounted in three triple turrets together with a relatively strong flak armament and four triple torpedo tubes. The development was the forerunner of the *Panzerschiffe*, or pocket-battleships, packing the greatest possible punch with the ability to absorb punishment. The speed of 32kt was equivalent to the best for the period. Range was poor, but was improved by the addition of a cruise diesel during construction. This afterthought produced technical problems which led to a third shaft for the diesel drive being fitted aboard *Leipzig* and *Nürnberg* .

Efforts to save weight and keep the ships within Treaty limitations resulted in the sides, decks, bulkheads and frames of the three 'K' class cruisers being on the thin side. Fractures and tears amidships followed passage in heavy seas or when the guns were fired, and the problem had not been eradicated by the time *Leipzig* and *Nürnberg* entered service.

Differences in hull form and the arrangement of weapons and machinery of the 'K' class in comparison with *Emden* illustrate how the latter was essentially a ship of the old Imperial Navy *Cöln* class while the 'K' class represented a fresh development altogether. *Emden*'s length-to-beam ratio was 10.6, that of the *Königsberg* class 11.12. The long, flat aftership of the latter ended with an inclined stern. *Leipzig* and *Nürnberg* were shorter on the waterline and the length-to-beam ratio was 10.17. The draught was shallower and the last two ships had a cruiser stern.

As regards the choice of calibre, the victorious powers allowed 15cm guns but forbade pairing off in twin turrets aboard *Emden*, so they were eventually mounted singly in old gunhouses. Over the next few years the prohibition seems to have fallen away and the 'K' class were fitted with nine 15cm guns in three triple turrets. In addition to advantages of ammunition storage and supply, compared to four twin turrets there was a weight saving leading to a reduction in the overall length and belt armour, which was in turn a further weight saving.

Leipzig and Nürnberg

These last two ships, designed in 1927 and 1933 respectively by Chief Naval Architect Blechschmidt, exhausted Germany's allowance of light cruisers under the Versailles Treaty. As usual, both were built to the longitudinal bulkhead system, the hulls being 90 per cent welded, with a double bottom length of 83 per cent. The displacement infringed Treaty limitations considerably, whereas that of the 'K' class had been only marginally in excess. The usual excuse—that the extra weight was only the armour—was offered, although the fact that the extra weight was also equivalent to that of all the guns was not mentioned. Both ships were shorter on the waterline and beamier than the 'K' class. The broader beam made a different arrangement possible for the engine room: for the same number of boilers there were just three boiler rooms, so that all gas flues could be trunked together into one funnel (the 'K' class, with four boiler rooms, had two funnels). The form of the main frame also differed: the armour deck of the 'K' class ran from side to side and met the upper edge of the belt armour, whereas on *Leipzig* the armour deck curved down short of the sides to meet the belt armour inside the lateral bulges. This was even more marked on *Nürnberg*. A new feature of these last two light cruisers was the central shaft for diesel drive, which was designed to overcome the difficulty aboard the 'K' class wherein drive had to be either turbine or diesel but not both simultaneously.

By the time *Nürnberg* was complete, the advantages of the 1935 Anglo-German Naval Agreement were already being enjoyed to the full. For example, the weight of the fire direction system alone was greater than the weight of all *Emden*'s guns at commissioning, and displacement was up by 130 tons over *Leipzig*. About 80 tons of this was compensated for by less bunkerage. Cabling accounted for 50 tons and provided numerous switching possibilities for the guns in any eventuality, although history proved this to have been an entirely unnecessary innovation.

The initial difficulties and breakdowns involving *Leipzig*'s diesel machinery and that of the gunnery training motor ship *Bremse* led to many erroneous conclusions being drawn. The high-pressure/hot-steam lobby took full advantage of the confusion. The *Kriegsmarine* turned its back on diesel drive for large ships for the critical period, and it was not until 1938 that realisation dawned that the German Navy had taken a false path.

Data

Emden

Building Details

Approved	1921 Naval Estimates
Builder	Marine Werft, Wilhelmshaven
Yard number	100
Contract placed	7.4.1921
Keel laid	8.12.1921
Launched	7.1.1925
Commissioned	15.10.1925

Measurements

Gross registered tons	4,844
Net registered tons	2,464
Displacement (standard)	5,600 tons
Displacement (designed)	6,056 tons
Displacement (operational)	6,990 tons
Length (waterline)	150.5m
Length (overall)	155.1m
Beam	14.3 m
Draught (designed)	5.15m
Draught (operational, maximum)	5.93m
Draught (based on std disp.)	5.38m
Height of sides	8.96m
Increase in draught per cm	17.3 tonnes
Length/beam ratio	10.6
Beam/draught ratio	2.68

Main Armament

8 × 15cm SK/L45 in single gunhouses, replaced in 1942 by TK-15 destroyer-type gunhouses. (Original scheme with IW5 barrels in four twin turrets not approved by NIACC.) Magazine capacity 60 rounds. Maximum range 17.6km. Maximum elevation 40°. Maximum depression –10°.

Secondary Armament

2 (later 3) × 8.8cm/L45 single-mounted flak/C32, magazine 1,200 rounds; from 1938/1943 additionally 4 × 3.7cm single-mounted flak/C30 plus two 20mm quadruples and 3–7 × 20mm MG/C30 singles. According to unconfirmed crew reports, in 1944 *Emden* received 3 × 10.5cm SKC/32gE flak to replace the three 8.8cm and was then also equipped with 2 × 4cm Flak 28 Bofors, 2 × 3.7cm Fl C/30U and 20 × 20mm Fl C/38.

Torpedoes and Mines

4 × 50cm tubes in twin mountings (8 × 53.3cm as originally designed, but not approved by NIACC). Torpedo stock from 1934: 12 torpedoes. Capacity for 120 mines.

Armour

Horizontal armour deck	20mm; 40mm over magazines
Armour deck slopes	20–40mm
Collision bulkhead	40mm
Ammunition supply shaft	20mm
Command tower (horizontal)	20mm
Command tower (vertical)	50mm
Command tower (companionway)	100mm
Main gunhouses	20mm
Belt armour amidships	50mm, decreasing towards the ends

Machinery

Six Schulz oil-fired single-ended boilers, heated surface 3,009m², and four Schulz coal-fired watertube boilers, operating pressure 16ats, heated surface 1,629m², these latter four converted to oil-firing in 1934 with heated surface 1,800m². Located in four boiler rooms.

Two BBC Mannheim turbine sets with wheel gearing, each set driving one shaft. Two turbine rooms. Two three-bladed propellers of 3.75m diameter. HP turbine 2,435rpm, LP turbine 1,568rpm. Shaft revolutions 295/min.

Auxiliary Machinery

Three 420 kW diesel generators.

Fuel Bunkerage

Coal 875 tonnes; heating oil 300m³ normal, 859m³ maxi-

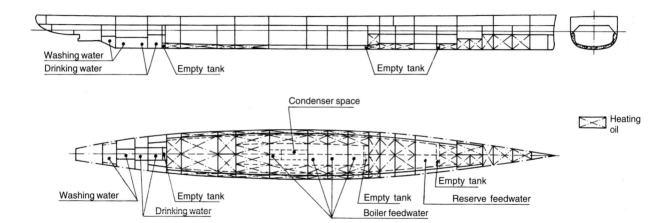

Washing water
Drinking water
Empty tank
Empty tank

Condenser space

Heating oil

Washing water
Empty tank
Empty tank
Drinking water
Boiler feedwater
Empty tank
Reserve feedwater

Above: *Emden*: arrangement of fuel bunkers after conversion to oil-firing.

mum; after conversion to pure oil-firing 1,266m³.
Range 5,290nm at 18kt, 6,750nm at 14kt. After conversion: 5,300nm at 18kt.
Designed rating 45,900shp at 295rpm for 29kt; maximum output at 46,500shp = 29.4kt. Performance weight per shp 28.1kgs.

MI weight (ship's machinery and electrical plant, inc. all auxiliary machinery, piping and cables) based on designed displacement = 1,290 tonnes.
MII weight (auxiliary boilers, rudder machinery, capstans, boats, aircraft cranes and communications systems) based on designed displacement = 248 tonnes.

Damage Control
Ring system of pumps passing through all important (battle) compartments. Two pumps with output of 600m³/hr. Two main 1,200m³/hr seawater cooling pumps for turbines could be linked in. Auxiliary pumping unit: 4 × 60m³/hr bilge pumps and one of 42m³/hr.

Other Information
One rudder. Six boats (later five, plus two motorised). Complement: 19 officers and 464 men (later 20 officers, 445 men and 162 cadets).

Königsberg Class

	Königsberg	*Karlsruhe*	*Köln*
Builder	Marinewerft, Wilhelmshaven	Deutsche Werke, Kiel	Marinewerft, Wilhelmshaven
Yard number	108	207	116
Laid down	12.4.26 as Cruiser 'B' (Replacement *Thetis*)	27.2.26 as Cruiser 'C' (Replacement *Medusa*)	7.8.26 as Cruiser 'D' (Repalcement *Arcona*)
Launched	26.3.27	20.8.27	23.5.28
Commissioned	17.4.29	6.11.29	15.1.30
Building costs (RM)	38m	36m (+ 5.7m for conversion at Wilhelmshaven)	36m
Measurement	5,475grt	5,433grt	5,342grt; 2,464nrt
Height of sides		9.25m	
Displacement (designed)		6,000 tons/6,750 tonnes (official)	

Displacement (operational)		7,700 tons	
After conversion (designed)	–	6,730 tons	–
After conversion (operational)	–	8,350 tons	–
Length (waterline)		169.0m	
Length (overall)		174.0m	
Beam		15.2m	
After conversion	–	16.8m	–
Draught		5.42m at 6,750 tons disp.	
		6.28m at 7,700 tons disp.	
		5.56m at 6,000 tons disp.	
After conversion	–	6.2m	–
Machinery output (turbines)	68,200shp	68,200shp	65,000/68,482shp
Machinery output (diesel)	1,800bhp	1,800bhp	1,800bhp
Propeller revolutions (turbines)	363rpm	371rpm	360/376rpm
After conversion	–	348prm	–
Speed (turbines)	32.1kt	32.1kt	32/32.5kt
Speed (cruising diesel)	10kt	10kt	10kt
Speed (after conversion)	–	30kt	–
Range(turbine drive)		5,700nm/19kt, 7,300nm/17kt	
Range (after conversion)	–	3,340nm/18kt	–
Range (diesels)	8,000nm/10kt (normal diesel oil bunker capacity; if all fuel bunkers aboard carried only diesel, range would have been about 18,000nm)		
Bunkerage (heating oil)	1,184m³ =1,100 tonnes, later increased to 1,300 tonnes (*Köln* 1,350 tonnes)		
Bunkerage (diesel)	261m³ = 139 tonnes, later increased to 150 tonnes (*Köln* finally 600 tonnes)		
After conversion	–	+ 110 tonnes heating oil	–
Ship's boats	8		
Crew	21 officers, 493 NCOs and men; as Flagship BdA* additionally 6 officers and 20 NCOs and men; later 23 officers and 588–591 NCOs and men; *Köln* finally 820–850 men		
Searchlights		5 each, 1.6m diameter	
Aircraft installation	From 1935 addition of a catapult and two aircraft, unshipped from *Köln* 1937. Later reinstalled as per *Karlsruhe* (1 × He 60C floatplane on catapult, the other dismantled below deck). From 1940 helicopter trials on *Köln*.		

Construction and Weight Groupings (*Köln*) (per Witte)

Length (construction waterline) (m)	169.00	Coefficient, fineness of waterplane (α)	0.70
Beam (m)	15.2	Longitudinal prismatic coefficient (δ)	0.47
Draught (m)	5.7	Midships section coefficient (β)	0.78
Designed displacement (tonnes)	6,752	Ratio δ/α	0.68
Length/beam ratio	11.11†	Ratio δ/β	0.61
Beam/draught ratio	2.81		
Freeboard aft (m)	3.95		
Freeboard forward (m)	8.00		
Length/height ratio	18.3		

The longitudinal prismatic coefficient is the ratio of the volume of displacement to the volume of a prism having a length equal to the length between perpendiculars and a cross-sectional area equal to the midship sectional area. The fineness of waterplane coefficient is the ratio of the

---

* BdA (*Befehlshaber der Aufklürungsstreitkräfte*) = Commanding Admiral Naval Scouting Forces. This Imperial Navy term for small cruisers persisted. BdK (*Befehlshaber der Kreuzer*) = Commanding Admiral Heavy Cruisers.

† *Karlsruhe* after conversion had a length-to-beam ratio of 10.06.

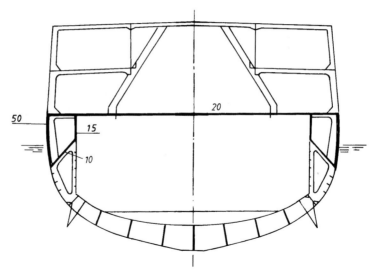

Above: Main frame, *Königsberg* class.

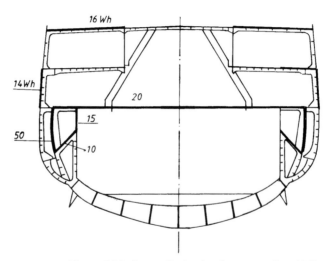

Above: Main frame, *Karlsruhe* after conversion, 1940.

area of the waterplane to the area of its circumscribing rectangle. The midship section coefficient is the ratio of the midship section area to the draught and breadth extreme amidships. The foregoing values of form were approximately the same for all three ships.

Weights (Building Steel ST45 and ST52)

SI plus barbettes (tonnes)	2,750
SII (metalworkers) (tonnes)	214
SIII (carpenters) (tonnes)	71
SIV (painters) (tonnes)	45
Total	3,080

Weight Groupings (as percentages)

Ship's hull	34
Armour	13
Main engines	22
Auxiliary machinery	4.5
Weapons	10.2
Equipment and consumables, crew, effects and provisions	4.5
Fresh and feedwater	2.8
Fuel	7.5
Reserve	1.5
Total	100

Leipzig and *Nürnberg*

	Leipzig	*Nürnberg*
Builder	Marinewerft, Wilhelmshaven	Deutsche Werke, Kiel
Order placed	1928	16.3.33
Yard number	117	234
Laid down	18.4.28 as Cruiser 'E' (Replacement *Amazone*)	4.11.33 as Cruiser 'F' (Replacement *Nymphe*)
Launched	18.10.29	8.12.34
Commissioned	8.10.31	3.11.35
Building costs (RM)	38m	40m
Measurement	5,825grt; 1,815nrt	6,264grt; 1,958nrt
Height of sides	9.00m	9.00m
Displacement (type)	6,614 tonnes	7,150 tonnes
Displacement (designed)	7,385 tonnes	8,060 tonnes
Displacement (operational)	8,427 tonnes	9,040 tonnes
Displacement (official)	6,000 tons (6,750 tonnes)	6,000 tons (6,650 tonnes)
Length (waterline)	165.8m	170.0m
Length (overall)	177.1m	181.3m
Beam	16.3m	16.4m
Draught (designed waterline)	5.05m	4.75m
Draught (maximum)	5.69m	5.79m
Machinery output (turbines)	60,000/65,585shp	60,000/66,075shp
Machinery output (diesel)	12,400/12,600bhp	12,400/12,600bhp
Propeller revolutions	309/400rpm	291/400rpm
Speed (maximum, unforced, turbines)	31.9/32.0kt	32.0/32.3kt
Speed (diesel)	16.5kt	16.5kt
Range	3,780nm/15kt 2,980nm/21kt 2,220nm/27kt 940nm/32kt	3,280nm/15kt 2,260nm/21kt 1,700nm/27kt 922nm/29.9kt
Bunkerage	1,235m³ heating oil 348m³ diesel	1,152m³ heating oil 348m³ diesel
Ship's boats	8	8
Aircraft	1 catapult, 2 × He 60C floatplanes, one on catapult, the other dismantled below deck	
Crew	26 officers, 508 NCOs and men	
As flagship	+ 6 officers, 20 men	+ 17 officers, 66 men
Later	30 officers, 628 men	
Finally	24 officers, 826 men	26 officers, 870 men

Construction and Weight Groupings (per Witte)

Leipzig

Ship's hull (tonnes)	2,557
Armour (less turrets) (tonnes)	774
Main machinery (tonnes)	1,637
Auxiliary machinery (tonnes)	394
Guns and equipment (tonnes)	640
Torpedoes and equipment (tonnes)	56
Aircraft installation and equipment (tonnes)	20
General equipment (tonnes)	126
Nautical instruments (tonnes)	7
Masts and spars (tonnes)	9
Empty ship with equipment (tonnes)	6,220

Ammunition (tonnes)	164
Torpedoes (tonnes)	23
Consumables (tonnes)	43
Crew (tonnes)	51
Effects (tonnes)	42
Provisions (tonnes)	71

Type displacement (less fresh and washing water) (tonnes)	6,614
Drinking water (tonnes)	47
Washing water (tonnes)	56
Feedwater (tonnes)	100
Heating oil (tonnes)	500
Diesel oil (tonnes)	47
Lubricating oil (tonnes)	17
Aviation spirit (tonnes)	4

Designed displacement (tonnes)	7,385
Feedwater (tonnes)	98
Heating oil (tonnes)	581
Diesel oil (tonnes)	262
Lubricating oil (tonnes)	72
Fresh water reserve (tonnes)	29

Total displacement (tonnes)	8,427

Main weight groupings: *Leipzig*

Ship's hull (%)	54.2
MI	22.2
MII	5.3
Crew, effects, provisions	2.2
Equipment and consumables	2.2
Fresh and washing water	1.4
Feedwater	1.4
Fuel	7.8

MI = Main machinery and connections, condensers, gear couplings, shaft connections, propellers, auxiliary machinery, conduits and piping used in connection with the operation of the main machinery, exhaust/funnel cap, equipment, etc., boilers with armatures, and oil and water in the main engine plant.

MII = Auxiliary boiler plant, ship's heating system, washing and drinking water desalination plant, laundry, ablutions, kitchen gear, etc., ship's pumps, primary electrical plant, lighting, cables, steering assembly, capstans, boats' windlasses, room fans, weapons systems, refrigerating plant, searchlights, signal lamps, command elements, gyro compass, mileage logs, sirens and workshops.

Main weight groupings: *Leipzig*

SI plus SII–IV (tonnes)	2,557
Equipment, consumables, crew, effects (tonnes)	481
Armour (less turret armour) (tonnes)	774
Main machinery (MI plus equipment) (tonnes)	1,637
Fuel and lubricating oil plus feedwater (tonnes)	1,681
Auxiliary machinery (MII plus equipment) (tonnes)	394
Weapons with equipment and ammunition (tonnes)	903

Designed displacement (tonnes)	7,385
Full displacement (tonnes)	8,427

SI (ST52 and ST45 plus armour and barbettes (tonnes)	774
SII = Metalworkers (tonnes)	1,886
SIII = Caprenters (tonnes)	55
SIV = Painters (tonnes)	50

Weight of ship (tonnes)	3,331

S = weight of compartmented hull – SI = building steel and turret armour, but not waterline armour, plus SII–IV.

Construction details: *Nürnberg*

Length/beam ratio (*Leipzig* 10.17)	10.43
Beam/draught ratio	3.44
Longitudinal prismatic coefficient (δ)	0.52
Coefficient, fineness of waterplane (α)	0.71
Midship section coefficient (β)	0.85
Ratio δ/α	0.74
Ratio δ/β	0.62

Armour

The armour of the three 'K' class cruisers was of the then current international standard for light cruisers and similar to the material used prior to World War I for 'protected small cruisers' but improved in the light of war experience and new alloys. Cuts in armour were made to keep the three ships within the 6,000-ton Washington Treaty weight limit. An armour deck 20–40mm thick and lacking the usual slope stretched across the beam from side to side. A 20mm collision bulkhead was positioned well forward. The so-called torpedo bulkhead was 15mm thick. The 50–70mm belt armour stretched lengthwise from 'C' turret to a point about 30m short of the stem, and the citadel area was enclosed within 70mm bulkheads at each end. All faces of the 15cm turrets were protected by 20–30mm armour. The barbettes were given 30mm and the command tower had thicknesses from 30 to 100mm.

During her conversion *Karlsruhe* was given a second outer skin of *wotan hart* 10–14mm plate and a new upper deck 16mm thick of the same material. There were four magazines. Two magazines, below the armour deck and platform deck respectively, served 'A' turret; Nos 3 and 4 magazines below the armour deck served 'B' and 'C' turrets respectively.

The armour scheme in *Leipzig* and *Nürnberg* differed little from that in the three earlier ships but was better arranged. The material—Krupp nickel-steel Pz240—was the best for the time: wotan hard and soft did not become available until *Nürnberg* was building, and this ship was in consequence better protected.

The maximum deck armour was 20mm thick (25mm at the slopes) while the battlemast had 30mm, 50mm and 100mm. Belt armour at the designed waterline varied from 18mm to 50mm, and the turrets had similar protection to the three earlier ships. In *Nürnberg* there were small differences: the shaft to the command tower was 60mm, the forward rangefinder 15mm, the foretop 20mm and the flak fire control 14mm. The 15cm turret had a greater thickness of armour, as did the barbettes (60mm) and their foundations (30mm).

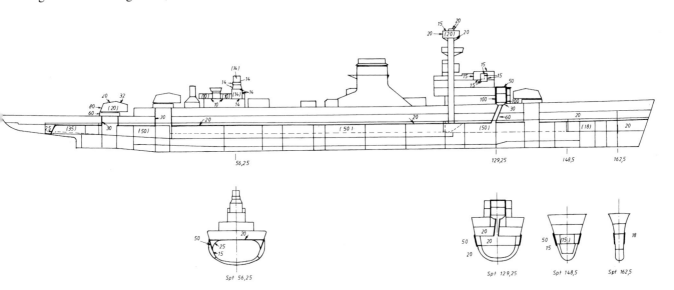

Above: *Nürnberg*: arrangement of armour. Thicknesses in mm.

Armament

The main armament of the 'K' class cruisers consisted of nine 15cm SK C/25 guns in three triple turrets on LC/25 turntable chassis. Flak calibres initially were 8.8cm, 3.7cm and 2cm. There were twelve 53.3cm torpedo tubes.

Main Armament: 15cm SK/L60 – C/25

SK = *Schnell-lade/Schnellfeuerkanone* (quick-loading/quick-firing gun). L = length of gun barrel expressed in multiples of calibre; thus 15cm/L60 = barrel length of 900cm.

Calibre	149.1mm
Muzzle velocity	960ms
Barrel length	60cal/9.08m
Length of barrel lining	57.5cal/8.57m
Length of breech chamber	1.39m
Designed gas pressure	3.85 atmospheres
Volume of breech chamber	27.7m³
Barrel life	500 rounds
Recoil energy at 0° elevation	52 tonnes
Length of grooving	7.067m
Depth of grooves	1.75mm
Type of grooves	Parabolic, 45/30cal
Width of grooves	6.14mm
No of grooves	44
Weight of breech and barrel	11.97 tonnes
Maximum range	25,700m

Chassis

Barrel elevation/depression	+40°/–10°
Rotation	±360° = 720°
Powered elevation speed	6°/sec
Powered rotation speed	6–8°/sec
Weight of gun cradles	2.44 tonnes
Weight of gun beds	54.26 tonnes
Weight of sighting equipment	3.5 tonnes
Weight of electrical machinery	11.12 tonnes
Weight of turret armour	24.8 tonnes
Total weight	136.91 tonnes
Armour	Front 30mm, sides 20mm, roof 20mm; material steel 420

Ammunition

Weight of projectile	45.5kg
Weight of charge (nose-fused)	3.892kg
Weight of charge (base-fused)	3.058kg
Weight of charge (AP)	0.885kg (Fp 02)
Filling	Fp 02
Length of projectile (base-fused)	4.5cal = 680mm
Length of projectile (nose-fused)	4.5cal = 655mm
Length of projectile (AP)	3.7cal = 555mm
Weight of cartridge case	33.4kg
Length of cartridge case	1,192mm
Propellant	20.4kg RPC/32 or RPC/38*
Detonator	C/27

Shell Characteristics
(From files and *Guidelines for Determining Ranges for Engagements and Choice of Shell*, OKM 1940)

Range (hm)†	Barrel elevation (°)	Impact velocity (ms)	Impact angle (°)
50	1.7	673	2.2
100	5.3	445	8.8
150	11.5	318	23.5
200	21.4	314	42
250	36	332	59.5

Range 25,700m with 19.3kg propellant C/32.
At 10° elevation, range 14,100m.
Nose-fused shells could penetrate a 60mm thickness of armour at 3,200m and 20mm at 11,200m.

* RPC/38 = *Rauchpulver 1938*, powder type and its year of manufacture.
† A hectometre, one-tenth of a kilometre, was the usual range measurement factor in German gunnery. To avoid confusion, however, ranges have generally been expressed as kilometres and fractions of kilometres elsewhere in this book.

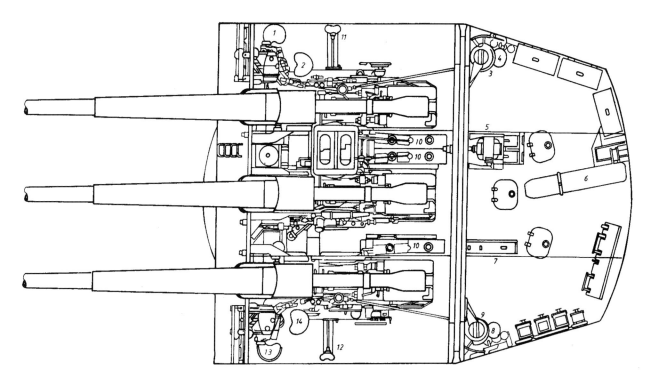

Above: 15cm C/25 SK/L60 in triple turret with turntable chassis C/25.
Key: 1. Gunner, indirect fire, traverse. 2. Gunner, direct fire, traverse. 3 and 9. Periscopes. 4 and 8. Turret commander.
5 and 7. Auxiliary ammunition lifts. 6. Cartridge ejection gear. 10. Main ammunition lift. 11. Target recognition crewman. 12. Lock
crewman. 13. Gunner, indirect fire, aimer. 14. Gunner, direct fire, aimer.

Differences in *Nürnberg*
Chassis

Powered barrel elevation	6–8°/sec
Powered rotation speed	7.6°/sec
Weight of gun cradles	2.457 tonnes
Weight of foundations	4.23 tonnes
Weight of gun beds	55.54 tonnes
Weight of sights	4.42 tonnes
Weight of electrical machinery	12.5 tonnes
Weight of turret armour	31.5 tonnes
Total weight	147.15 tonnes
Armour	Front 80mm, sides 20mm, roof 20–35mm, rear wall 35mm

The after turrets of the *Königsberg* class ships were situated off-centre, 'B' to port and 'C' to starboard of the centreline. This was to enable both rear turrets to be traversed to fire much finer over the bow during a pursuit. Theoretically it was quite a good idea but in practice the muzzle blast would probably have damaged the ship's superstructure. The normal centreline arrangement was restored for the two later ships.

Flak*

The 8.8cm L/75 C/25 flak on the C/25 double chassis was characterised by barrels wide-set due to the high axis stabiliser and external fuse gear. Speed of elevation or traverse was too slow at 10°/sec (although the later 10.5cm flak was even slower). The weapon was tested aboard *Köln* and found unsatisfactory after which the class received two 3.8cm L/45 on a C/13 central pivoting chassis. From 1933 *Köln* had four and from about 1935 *Königsberg* only two of these flaks, but from 1935–36 *Köln* and *Karlsruhe* had six. In 1940 *Königsberg* received six more weapons of this type. During her conversion *Karlsruhe* exchanged

---

* The term 'flak', a contraction of *Fliegerabwehrkanone*, is used throughout this book to describe German anti-aircraft (AA) weapons.

her 8.8cm flak for the 10.5cm twin flak which was then in general service with Fleet units.

The three 'K' class cruisers each had eight 3.7cm L/83 C/30 flak on C/30 double chassis and eight 2cm L/65 C/38 on C/30 single mountings. For 1945 it was planned to fit aboard *Köln*—the only survivor of the class after April 1940—ten 3.7cm and twenty-four 2cm kgC/28 in twin mountings, but in the end she received eight of the former, eighteen of the latter and four Bofors (28) 4cm. There were unfulfilled plans for ten 3.7cm 43M and twelve 2cm LM44 twins.

Flak aboard *Leipzig* initially comprised two 8.8cm L/45, increased by two in 1934 and finally replaced by six twin-mounted 2cm L/76. From 1941 until about October 1944 she was equipped with eight 3.7cm and fourteen 2cm flak; at the end this had been supplemented by four more 3.7cm and eight more 2cm.

On entering service *Nürnberg* carried eight 8.8cm L/76 and eight 3.7cm, both on double chassis. Her inventory of 2cm flak was varied upwards regularly.

As with all navies of the time, shipboard anti-aircraft armament was generally inadequate in the *Kriegsmarine*. Even the Royal Navy admitted that the aerial danger had been underestimated. US Navy exercises early on had provided reliable evidence, and the Spanish Civil War also indicated the danger, and it was the latter experience which persuaded the Royal Navy to convert their 'C' class light cruisers into AA cruisers. By the outbreak of war a considerable number of these AA ships were in service, and many merchant vessels were also provided with anti-aircraft weapons.

The British considered that heavy AA guns were inadequate and favoured lighter-barrelled models. Not until the loss of *Königsberg* to British dive-bombers did the realisation of the danger of bombs and aerial torpedoes finally dawn in Germany. There was a relatively fast re-think about defences and a handful of antiquated cruisers and prizes were converted into flak ships. Perhaps it would have been a good idea to have followed the British example and added *Emden*, *Köln*, *Leipzig* and *Nürnberg* to their numbers.

8.8cm Flak L/45 in MPL C/13

Calibre	88mm
Muzzle velocity	790ms
Recoil energy at 0° barrel elevation	13.2 tonnes
Weight of breech and barrel	2.5 tonnes
Weight of shell	9kg
Weight of propellant	2.35kg

8.8cm SKC/32 L/76 on twin-mounted C/32

Calibre	88mm
Muzzle velocity	950ms
Length of barrel	76cal/6.69m
Length of barrel lining	72cal/6.34m
Designed gas pressure	3.15 atmospheres
Barrel life	3,200 rounds
Recoil energy at 0° barrel elevation	7.8 tonnes
Weight of breech and barrel	3.64 tonnes
Maximum range (surface target)	17,200m
Maximum range (aerial target)	12,400m

Chassis

Barrel elevation	±80°/–10°
Rotation	±360° = 720°
Manual gun elevation	3.6°/sec
Powered gun elevation	10°/sec
Weight of gun cradle	1.775 tonnes
Weight of bed	0.815 tonnes
Weight of chassis	6.275 tonnes
Weight of sights	0.745 tonnes
Weight of electrical motor	1.28 tonnes
Weight of splinter shield	5.83 tonnes
Total weight of chassis	23.65 tonnes
Armour protection	Front 12mm, sides 10mm
Armour material	Wotan hard (WhnA)

Ammunition

Weight of projectile	9kg
Weight of charge	3.1kg
Length of projectile	0.397m
Total weight of projectile	15 kg (with length of 0.932m)

3.7cm SKC/30 twin-mounted C/30

Calibre	37mm
Muzzle velocity	1,000ms
Muzzle energy	38 megatonnes
Length of barrel	83cal/3.074m
Length of barrel lining	80cal/2.96m
Designed gas pressure	3.45 atmospheres
Barrel life	7,500 rounds
Recoil energy at 0° elevation	1 tonne
Length of grooves	2.554m
Type of grooves	Cubic parabola 50/35
Number of grooves	16
Weight of breech and barrel	243kg
Maximum range (surface target)	8,500m

Maximum range (aerial target)	6,800m
Maximum range (tracer)	4,800m

Ammunition

Weight of shell	0.742kg
Weight of charge	0.365kg
Filling	Fp 02
Length of shell	0.162m
Weight of cartridge case	0.97kg
Length of cartridge	0.381m
Propellant	RPC/32
Total weight	2.1kg
Total length	0.5165m
Fuse	Nose fuse E C/30
	Nose fuse C/34
	Tracer C/34
Burning period of tracer	12sec
Rate of fire	160 rds/barrel/min (theoretical), 80 rds/barrel/min (in practice)

Chassis

Barrel elevation	+85°/–10°
Rotation	±360° = 720°
Manual elevation	3°/sec
Manual rotation	4°/sec
Weight of rotatable unit	243kg
Weight of cradle	71kg
Weight of bed	2.162 tonnes
Weight of sights	87kg
Weight of electrical drive	630kg
Total weight	3.67 tonnes

2cm Flak C/30 on C/30 chassis

Calibre	20mm
Muzzle velocity	835ms
Barrel length	65cal/1.3m
Length of barrel lining	65cal/1.3m
Designed gas pressure	2.8 atmospheres
Barrel life	22,000 rounds
Recoil energy at 0° elevation	250kg
Length of grooving	720mm
Weight of breech and barrel	64kg
Maximum range (surface target)	4,900m
Maximum range (aerial target)	3,700m

Chassis

Barrel elevation	+85°/–11°

Weight of rotatable unit	43kg
Weight of chassis less sights	282kg
Total weight	420kg

Ammunition

Weight of projectile	134g
Length of projectile	78.5mm
Weight of charge	39.5g
Total weight	320g
Total length	203mm
Rate of fire	280rds/barrel/min (theoretical), 120 rds/barrel/min (in practice)

4cm Flak 28 (Bofors)

Calibre	40mm
Muzzle velocity	854ms
Barrel length	2.249m
Length of grooving	1.932m

Torpedoes

All five latter ships were equipped initially with twelve 50cm torpedo tubes mounted as four triple sets, two either side. The calibre was changed to 53.3cm in 1934. In 1940 one triple set aboard *Köln*, and in 1941 two sets aboard *Nürnberg*, were unshipped. In 1944 all tubes aboard *Leipzig* were dismounted.

Mines

Depending on the type of mine, all cruisers could carry up to 120 mines mounted on temporary rails aft.

Below: *Königsberg*'s main armament: 'B' and 'C' turrets.

Fire Control System

All five cruisers were supplied with three 6m rangefinders. These were located one each on the foretop and in the forward and after fire control positions (except *Köln* from 1939, when a rangefinding radar replaced the forward rangefinder.) Three 3m rangefinders were located one either side of the battlemast and the third in the after fire control position. These served the non-centralised flak and torpedo batteries. The equipment on *Leipzig* and *Nürnberg* was of an improved standard.

Radar

In 1904 Hillsmeyer lodged the first German patent for a primitive radar, but it was not until 15 January 1934 that the *Reichsmarine* carried out the first sea trial, aboard the auxiliary *Welle*. The unit worked on the 13.5cm frequency with an output of 300MW. Range was from two to four kilometres. A second trial aboard *Welle* on 24 October 1934 achieved a range of 12km. The equipment was not reliable, however, and the GEMA company was commissioned to build a set on the 50cm wavelength. This was fitted inside a box-shaped structure on *Köln*'s bridge and provided a fixed view of the area ahead of the ship. In trials on 26 September 1935 the gunnery training ship *Bremse* was pinpointed at a range of 8km. Aboard *Welle* later a landmass was picked out 20km distant. A 60cm wavelength development followed, which led in turn to the standard 81.5cm frequency unit known as *Seetakt* with an output of 368MHz. As with all German radar, it was plagued with problems caused by condensation and vibration. Five 60cm sets were ordered in 1937–38 and fitted experimentally aboard *Königsberg*, *Admiral Graf Spee*, the old torpedo-boat *G 10* and the trials boat *Strahl*. In 1938, 31 units of the 81.5cm prototype were ordered, and these were delivered between October 1939 and December 1940. They were known as 'DT I', then 'DT 101' and finally FuMG 39G(gL). Impulse output was 1kW, the keying frequency 1,000Hz (later 500Hz). The FuMG 39G(gL), known later as the FuMO 21, was earmarked for destroyers and, initially, the light cruisers. The dimensions of the characteristic 'mattress' were 1.9 × 4m. A model was fitted aboard *Nürnberg* in the summer of 1941.

Only *Köln* of the three 'K' class cruisers was given radar during the war. An FuMO 21 was fitted in place of the 6m rangefinder on the forward fire control platform. It is possible that it was replaced later by an FuMO 24/25. This latter unit worked on the 81.5cm wavelength and had a range of up to 20km (surface) or 30km (aerial). It was accurate to within 70m.

Leipzig received an FuMO 24/25 during repairs in August 1943, the 1.9 × 4m antenna being lodged on an outrigger on the forward face of the battlemast. On an arm above it was fitted an FuMB 6 *Palau* antenna, and at the side of the foretop *Sumatra* Fu MB4 aerials.

The FuMO 21 fitted on *Nürnberg* in 1941 was unshipped in the summer of 1944 and the position given over to flak. The ship was then equipped similarly to *Leipzig*, differences being that the *Sumatra* aerial was fixed on the foretop itself while the mainmast abaft the funnel was strengthened by a tripod base in order to carry a 2.2 × 2.4m FuMO 63 *Hohentwiel-K* aerial.

Below: A view from the foremast over *Königsberg*'s bridge, showing the 6m rangefinder for 'A' main turret.

Machinery

Königsberg Class

Six oil-fired Schulz-Thornycroft double-ended watertube boilers with natural circulation supplied the turbines' steam requirement. The boilers were located in four rooms with eight control stands. Rooms I and II were located in compartments VIII and IX respectively, each with two boilers trunked through the rear funnel; rooms III and IV, in compartments X and XI respectively, had one boiler apiece trunked through the forward funnel.

The total heating surface was $2 \times 1,250m^2$ plus $4 \times 1,010m^2 = 6,540m^2$, operating pressure 16 atmospheres. The four larger boilers had 22, the other pair 18 Körting burners. For the boilers in rooms I and II, steam production was 70 tonnes/hr, steam volume $5.8m^3$ and water volume $17.2m^3$; there were 3,600 tubes, and the boiler weight was 72 tonnes.

Each boiler room was fitted with one main and one reserve steam-driven feed pump, a feedwater pre-heater and an upper surface pre-heater built into the pressure pipes of the feedwater pump and heated by exhaust steam from the auxiliary machinery. The heating surface in boiler rooms I and II was about $78m^2$, and about $48m^2$ in boiler rooms III and IV. Boiler rooms I and II each had four, rooms III and IV each two ventilators worked by the turbines supplying air for combustion at the required pressure. This also helped maintain a good air flow in the boiler rooms and kept room temperatures tolerable. There were two 2-cylinder steam pumps in each boiler room to work the oil heating plant. The two forward boiler rooms each had two fuel oil pre-heaters and the after two rooms one each. These pre-heaters were normally heated by waste steam from the auxiliary machinery, although fresh steam directly from the boilers could also be used. A 2-cylinder pump forward and aft brought up fuel oil from the bunkers.

Drive Machinery

The two propeller shafts were turned by two HP and two cruising geared turbine sets. The HP and cruising turbine set could work jointly or either one alone. The manufacturers were Schichau for *Königsberg*, Krupp Germania for *Karlsruhe* and Blohm & Voss for *Köln*.

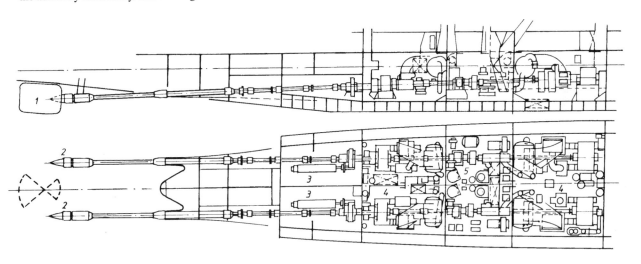

Above: *Königsberg* class: Arrangement of turbine and diesel powerplant.
Key: 1. Rudder. 2. Shafts. 3. Cruising diesels. 4. Turbine rooms. 5. Auxiliary machinery room.

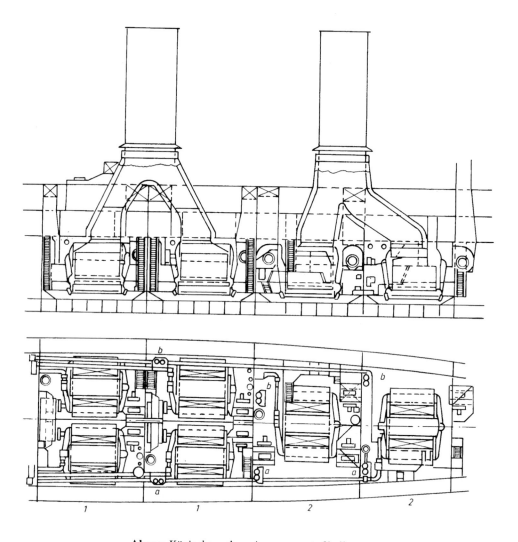

Above: *Königsberg* class: Arrangement of boilers.
Key: 1. Two double-ended boilers. 2. One double-ended boiler. a. Main feed pump. b. Reserve feed pump.

The turbine plant was distributed over four rooms, two each side of a longitudinal bulkhead. The two HP turbines sets were housed in compartment VII forward and the LP turbine sets in compartment V further aft. The HP main turbine aboard *Karlsruhe* had cruising stages disengaged at high loadings. The reversing turbines were integrated into the housing of the LP turbines. The ships' maximum speed was 32kt at 370rpm, and the maximum forced endurance speed 29kt at 310rpm.

Cruising Diesel

In addition to the main turbines the three ships were fitted with a MAN Type W10 V 26/33 reversible, compression-free, 10-cylinder, 4-stroke, 900PSe/1,600shp cruising die-sel with a cylinder diameter of 260mm, a piston stroke of 330mm, an average piston speed of 9.9ms, an average effective pressure of 1.15kg/cm^2, an output per litre of 5.13PSe and an output of 5.5kg/PSe at 900rpm.* These were extremely lightly built motors designed for another purpose and not included in the original building plans: they had proved so successful and reliable on the test bench that it was decided to include them as an afterthought. The weight increase was not great, and the motors extended the ships' radius of action and guaranteed an economic cruising performance, if only at 10.5kt. There was little space avail-

---

* Unless otherwise stated, the German term 'PSe' (*Pferdestärke* = diesel horsepower) has been left as original (1PSe = 0.9860hp).

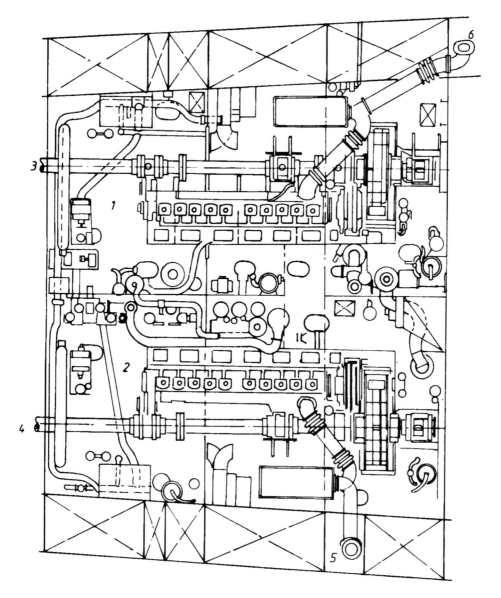

Above: *Königsberg* class: Diesel plant.
Key: 1. Diesel engine port. 2. Diesel engine starboard. 3. Port shaft. 4. Starboard shaft. 5. Starboard exhaust. 6. Port exhaust.

able in the stern, and the unit was eventually squeezed into compartment IV. At high speed the motors were dead weight as they could not be double-coupled with the turbines to drive the shafts. Motor output to the shafts was transferred through a Vulcan reduction gear.

Rudder and Propeller

The ships were equipped with a single rudder. Each of the two shafts had a three-bladed iron-bronze propeller, counter-rotating (starboard turning clockwise, port anti-clockwise). Propeller diameters were 4.1m for *Königsberg*, 3.35m for *Köln* and 3.4m for *Karlsruhe*. From the tables it will be noticed that, despite a slightly lesser maximum engine output (68,350shp against 68,485shp), a higher speed—32.461kt as against 32.278kt—was obtained with the smaller propeller. All mileage trials were held off Neukrug with a bottom of 60–65m. The weather was good, with sea state 2 and wind strength 3–4. *Karlsruhe*'s trials were held in January 1930 and those of *Köln* in April (with the 4.1m propeller) and May 1930 (3.7m propeller).

Diesel trials were very satisfactory, speeds of 10–10.5kt being recorded for 94–97rpm. Only the total fuel consumption could be estimated on these trials. The workshop tests resulted in a specific consumption of 180–185g/PSe.

Rpm/shaft	Output (shp)	Speed (kt)	Apparent slip (%)
Karlsruhe			
109.4	2,305	11,522	4.36
158.6	6.070	16,704	4.4
201.5	11,680	21,067	5.08
251.4	23,685	25,708	7.2
298.7	40,340	29,242	11.16
351.0	60,830	31,733	17.97
362.5	68,200	32,155	19.48

Köln (4.1m propeller)			
90.7	1,378	9.486	3.56
139.7	4,140	14.53	3.74
226.5	17,180	23.021	6.32
261.9	26,250	26.197	7.73
316.7	44,455	29.375	14.49
348.1	57,250	31.005	17.85
377.9	68,485	32.278	21.28

Köln (3.7m propeller)			
71.1	624	7.482	11.09
113.9	2,073	11.923	10.77
162.6	6,365	17.306	10.01
210.2	13,005	21.946	11.73
223.5	16,330	23.523	11.90
253.9	23,995	26.093	13.08
318.0	47,385	30.329	19.34
341.3	56,775	31.400	22.21
369.4	68,350	32.461	25.68

Leipzig and *Nürnberg*

Although similar in general to the 'K' class powerplant, substantial differences included the addition of a central shaft served excusively by the diesel.

Boilers

Six double-ended watertube boilers with natural circulation were located in three boiler rooms, the aftermost of which had a heating surface of 1,054m² with eighteen boilers each of 2.5mm bore. The forward rooms each had a 926m² heating surface with sixteen burners. The total heating surface in *Leipzig* was 2,906m² and in *Nürnberg* 5,510m². The operating pressure was 16 atmospheres (*Nürnberg* 17), the maximum fuel consumption 7.2 tonnes/hr, the maximum steam production 72 tonnes/hr, the heating surface loading about 6.85kg fuel/m² producing about 70kg steam/m² heating surface, the weight of boiler, jacket and fittings 47.41 tonnes, the water content at 0°C 14.67 tonnes and the total boiler weight 62.24 tonnes.

Turbine Machinery

Although the turbines were of uniform type (*Leipzig*'s manufactured by Krupp Germania and *Nürnberg*'s by Deutsche Werke, Kiel), many difficulties were caused by the variety of auxiliary machinery which had resulted, during the period when *Leipzig* was being built, from the efforts made at that time to broaden the base of industrial production in Germany. On these two ships the diesels could be coupled up with the turbines so that all three shafts turned at the same time.

Aboard *Leipzig* each turbine set consisted of an HP and a dual-flow LP turbine with a two-stage Curtis wheel. The reverse turbine had a two-stage Curtis wheel and four pressure stages. The transmission ratio was 1:795.

Aboard *Nürnberg* each turbine set consisted of an HP turbine and two LP turbines, with the unusual feature of having a condenser attached. Each turbine set produced 33,000hp and weighed 79.5 tonnes. The drive machinery weighed 35.25 tonnes, and turbine output was 3.48kg/hp.

Diesels

Whereas the two shafts of the 'K' class were turned either by turbine drive or diesels as selected and not both together, a third, central shaft aboard *Leipzig* and *Nürnberg* enabled the turbines to work the two outer shafts and the diesel to drive the central propeller in unison. A light cruiser with three screws was unusual. Where one of the two methods of propulsion had been disengaged and it was required to double-couple, all shafts had to be brought to a standstill for about ten minutes while the change was made. In wartime this was a calculated risk. Although not directly the cause of the collision, in October 1944 *Leipzig* had been adrift in the swept channel off Gotenhafen for ten minutes while the turbines were coupled in. A few minutes after resuming, she was rammed by the heavy cruiser *Prinz Eugen* in mist and darkness. (See section under *Leipzig* for further details). The great advantage of the diesels was that they replaced the cruising turbines.

Leipzig's plant comprised four MAN M7 Zu 30/44 double-acting, 7-cylinder, two-stroke diesels without compression. Cylinder diameter was 300mm, piston hub 440mm and motor revolutions 600rpm, and average piston speed was 8.8ms, average effective pressure 5.7kg/cm^2 and efficiency per litre 7.38PSe. There were also two MAN M7 Z23/34 auxiliary motors, cylinder diameter 230mm, piston hub 340mm, revolutions 750rpm and average effective pressure 4kg/cm^2. *Nürnberg*'s plant was similar but the motor type was MAN M7 Zu 32/44, cylinder diameter 320mm, piston hub 440mm and average effective pressure 4.9kg/cm^2. *Nürnberg*'s two auxiliary motors were of the same type as *Leipzig*'s but had an output of 1,450PSe and 725rpm and an average effective pressure of 4.75kg/cm^2.

The diesels for *Nürnberg* were supplied in February 1935 and were an improved version of those installed aboard *Leipzig* following an anti-diesel campaign by the pro-turbine lobby. There had been difficulties with the plants installed aboard *Leipzig* and the gunnery training ship *Bremse*, but these were in the nature of things. Diesels were an innovation aboard large warships and had to be of the lightest possible construction with an eye to keeping the ship within Treaty limits.

The *Leipzig* diesels continued to be troublesome and the problems were not finally eradicated until the outbreak of war in 1939. A MAN document summarises the careers of the *Leipzig* and *Nürnberg* diesels:

Cruiser *Leipzig*
Modifications carried out on the cruising-diesel unit
General

Contract placed	27.3.28
Four motors	M7 Zu 30/44
Maximum output each motor	3,100PSe at 600rpm
Two auxiliary motors	M7 Z 23/34, 725rpm
Installation commenced	20.5.31
Commissioned	8.10.31
First diesel trials	9.5.32
Acceptance voyage	16.6.32

Refit (exchange of all cylinder centre parts and hubs for main and auxiliary motors, mercury suppressor)	13.11.33–12.2.34
Removal of motors	15.3.35
Refit (main and auxiliary motor piston shafts, drive rods, crossheads with nuts, both superchargers, all lubricating oil, cooling oil and seawater pumps	11.36–15.2.37
Exchange of three crankshafts from main and one auxiliary motor	12.38–3.39

A similar report was made out for *Leipzig*:

Cruiser *Leipzig*
Modifications made to cruising diesel unit
General

Contract placed	3.6.33
Four motors	M7 Zu 32/44
Output each motor	3,100PSe at 600rpm
Two auxiliary motors	M7 Z 23/34
Output each motor	1,450PSe at 725rpm
Launched	8.12.34
First trial	10.9.35
Termination of one-year guarantee	11.4.37

Cylinder hubs and jackets

On the test stand the zinc protection for the fresh water cooler hubs was not completed satisfactorily, the area affected being the inner surface of the cooling water jacket for the M Zu 32/44 motor. Post-zinc work will continue as scheduled 13.2.35. Zinc protection of the mantle affected was removed and the casing parkerised on waterside 16.3.35.

The diesels of both ships worked the central shaft through a Vulcan gearing, and the two cruisers were the first German warships of this size to have a controllable-pitch propeller, which, it was hoped, would provide a speed of 18kt for an output of 12,000hp on the central shaft and improve speed when used in conjunction with the turbines. There were two settings—2.3m for high speed, and 3.35m. The designed pitch was 2.65m. The *Leipzig* propeller was based on a design which had not previously been tested aboard ship. Although sound on the test bench, it was found impractical when fitted and eventually gave way to a fixed propeller. A similar unit aboard *Nürnberg* had been built at Wilhelmshaven and proved more satisfactory, although it had only two possible settings, high and cruising speed and the ship had to stop engines to make the adjustment. Therefore to vary the pitch of the propellers or couple up/decouple the central shaft, the shaft had to be stationary with the brake on. The propeller pitch could not be varied until the ship was making less than 10kt through the water. The whole procedure took about fifteen minutes—a severe drawback. In practice the system was not proven. A single rudder was fitted.

Electrical Installation

There were two electric motor rooms (*E-Werke*) located in compartments IV (*E-Werk I*, port and starboard) and XIII (*E-Werk III*, port and starboard), the units in each room being separated by dividing walls. The primary installation consisted of two 250kW turbo-generators of 3,000rpm and two 90 kW diesel generators of 1,300rpm. The four aggregates were spread over three control stations so that if an individual *E-Werk* flooded there would be no danger of a total failure of electrical supply (the war proved otherwise). The generators were 6-cylinder, four-stroke, simple working, air-injected Maybach motors supplying 220V DC. Cylinder diameter was 140mm, piston hub 180mm and endurance output 137.5PSe (maximum 150PSe). The diesel generator revolutions were high and motor output, at 7kg/PSe, low.

The installations aboard *Leipzig* and *Nürnberg* had a greater capacity than those on the three earlier cruisers.

Leipzig's comprised three electric motor rooms each with one turbo- and one diesel-generator of 180kW, *Nürnberg*'s four electric motor rooms each with two 300kW turbo-generators and two 350kW diesel generators.

Auxiliary Machinery

All ships were fitted with two desalination units in the auxiliary motor room and in compartment VI (starboard and port) below the armour deck, plus a third in the 'tween deck. Two oil-driven watertube boilers with a heating surface of 90m² were used in harbour or when using diesel drive alone.

The refrigerating unit—capable of producing five tonnes of ice hourly from water at 30°C—and magazines used carbonic acid for temperature stability. Magazine temperatures were maintained within the 0°–30°C range.

The rudders of each ship were served by one or two independent motors, depending on whether turbine or diesel drive was in use. A manual station was available if necessary.

All bow and stern capstans were electrically operated. Each ship carried one stern and three bow anchors lodged in side cluses (after her major refit the starboard bow anchor aboard *Karlsruhe* rested in a deck cluse). Bow anchors weighed 4 tonnes (the stern anchor was lighter by one-half to two-thirds), chain weight was 1,575kg, and length of chain 225m plus 75m reserve. For foreign cruises a 600kg kedge was carried for shallow-water anchoring and other uses.

Left: One of *Leipzig*'s double-action MAN M7Z 30/44 two-stroke diesel motors being assembled at the Augsburg-Nuremberg factory.
Right: *Leipzig* at the end of her career.

The *Spähkreuzer* Programme

On 27 January 1939 Hitler approved the gigantic naval building programme known as the Z-Plan. At the light cruiser level it was proposed to augment the existing six light cruisers with which this book deals by the addition of sixteen light cruisers of 8,000 tonnes displacement and 22 *Spähkreuzer* (reconnaissance cruisers) of 6,000 tonnes full load displacement.

The *Spähkreuzer* project began in March 1940 and was based on Type 1938 plans for the destroyers *Z 40–Z 42*. The *Spähkreuzer* were essentially scaled-up destroyers, larger and more heavily armed than the World War I cruiser *Emden*. The contract for SP-1, to the Blohm & Voss, Hamburg, design, was placed with Germania Werft, Kiel, on 17 February 1941 and the keel was laid on 20 August that year as Yard No 642. Machinery for all six vessels was ordered in December 1941, but the project was cancelled the same month and the keel material scrapped.

Spähkreuzer SP-1–SP-3

Displacement (standard)	5,037 tonnes
Displacement (full load)	5,900 tonnes
Length (overall)	152.2 m
Length (waterline)	145.0m
Beam	14.62 m
Draught	4.66m
Watertight compartments	17
Armament	6 × 15cm guns in three twin turrets; 4 × 8.8cm; 8 × 3.7cm, 12 × 2cm; ten torpedo tubes in five twin mountings;up to 50 mines
Machinery	Turbines (77,500shp) plus diesel (14,500hp)
Speed (turbines)	35.5kt
Bunkerage	850 tonnes
Range	8,000 nm at 17kt
Boats	5
Crew	18 officers, 520 men

Scale Drawings

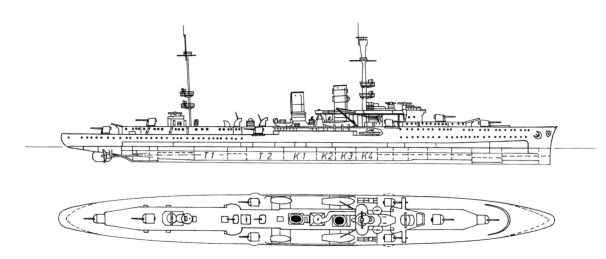

Above: *Emden* in 1926.
Key: T1 and T2 = turbine rooms; K1–K4 = boiler rooms.

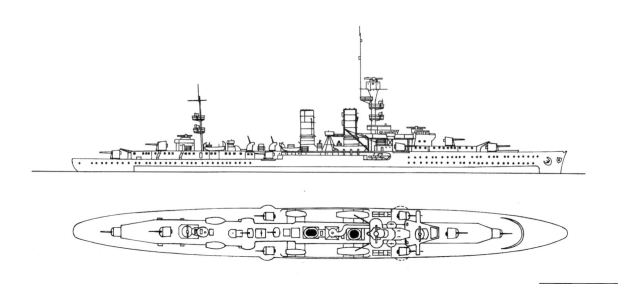

0 5 10 15 20 25

Above: *Emden*, 1926–34.

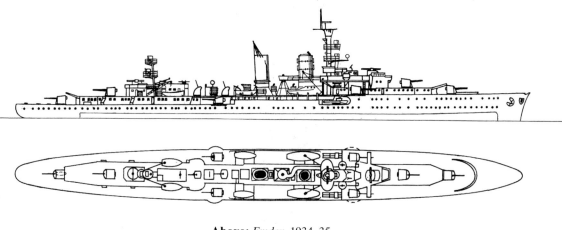

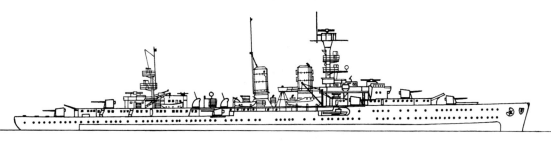

Above: *Emden*, 1934–35.

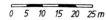

0 5 10 15 20 25 m

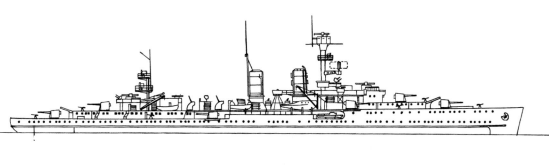

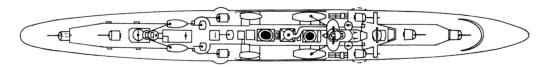

Above: *Emden*, 1935–42.
Bow heraldic shield removed on outbreak of war.

0 5 10 15 20 25 m

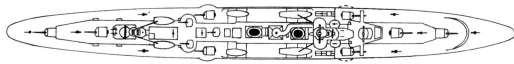

Above: *Emden*, 1942–45.
Note degaussing coil along hull.

0 5 10 15 20 25 m

Above: *Königsberg*: top, appearance about 1930; bottom, after 1939–40 refits.

0 5 10 15 20 m

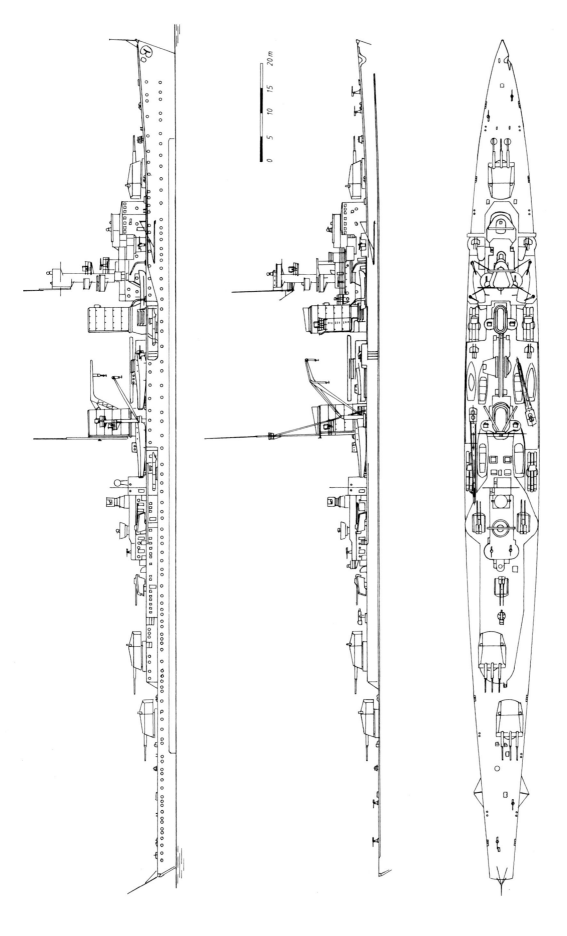

Above: *Karlsruhe*: top, about 1935–36; centre and bottom: after major refit 1939–40.

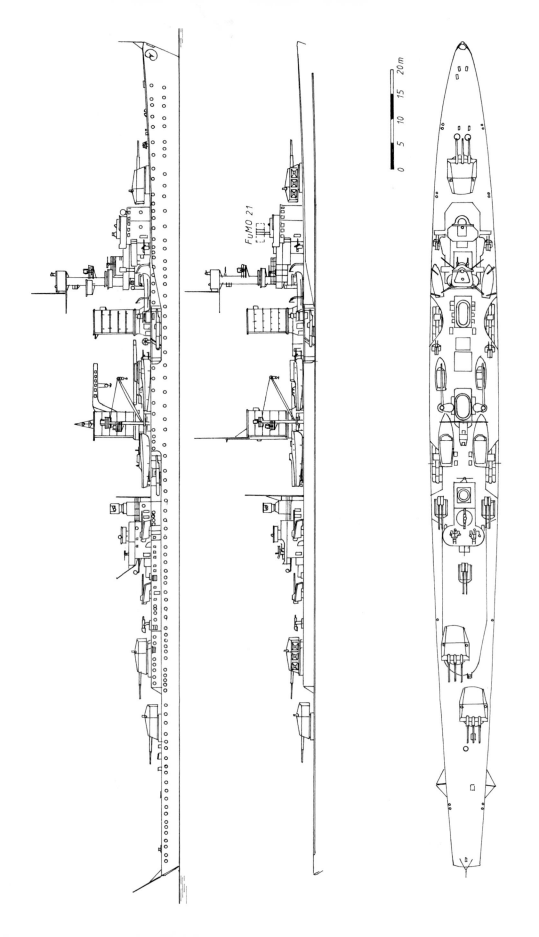

FuMO 21

Above: *Köln*: top, about 1935–36; centre and bottom: after modifications, from about 1941–42.

Above: *Köln*: camouflage scheme 1941–42, from a sketch copied from a photograph taken against the light, which makes the hull appear darker than usual.

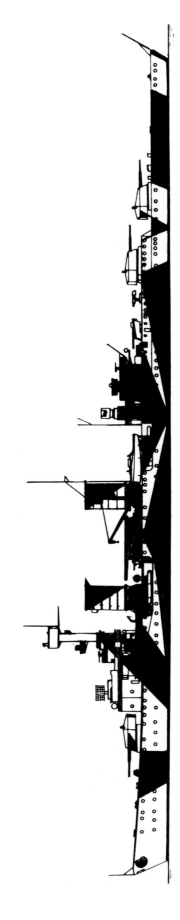

Above: *Köln*: camouflage scheme, 1943.

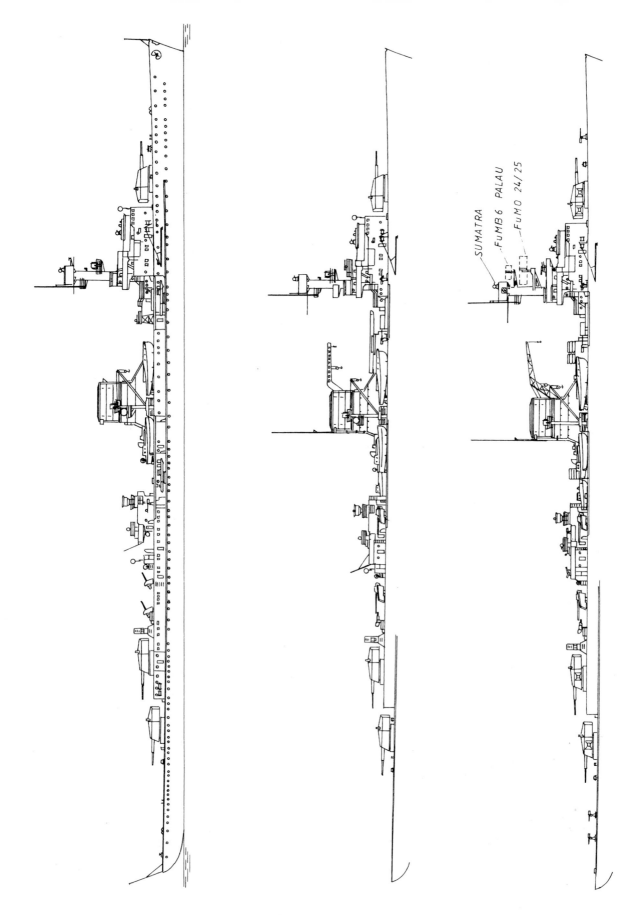

Above: *Leipzig*: top, appearance about 1933; centre, after modifications, about 1936; bottom, as in 1943–44.

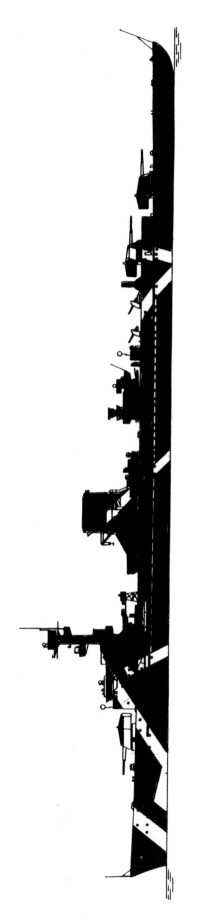

Above: *Leipzig*: camouflage scheme, 1941.

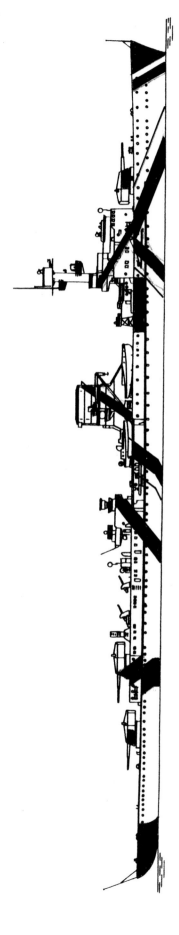

Above: *Leipzig*: camouflage scheme, 1941–42.

Principal alterations after outbreak of war:

a) Rangefinder atop forward fire control replaced by FuMO 21.

b) FuMO 21 exchanged for FuMO 24 or 25 on outrigger from battlemast, with FuMB 6 above; FuMO 21 position occupied by flak mounting.

c) Additional pole added to mainmast to carry FuMO 63; generally more flak positions and *Sumatra* antennas.

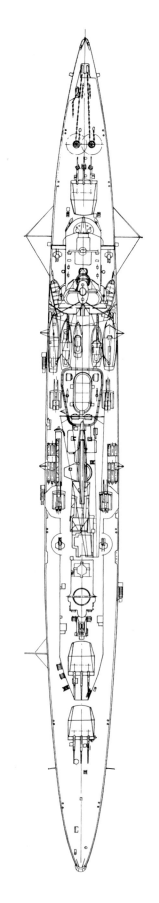

Above: *Nürnberg:* appearance on commissioning.

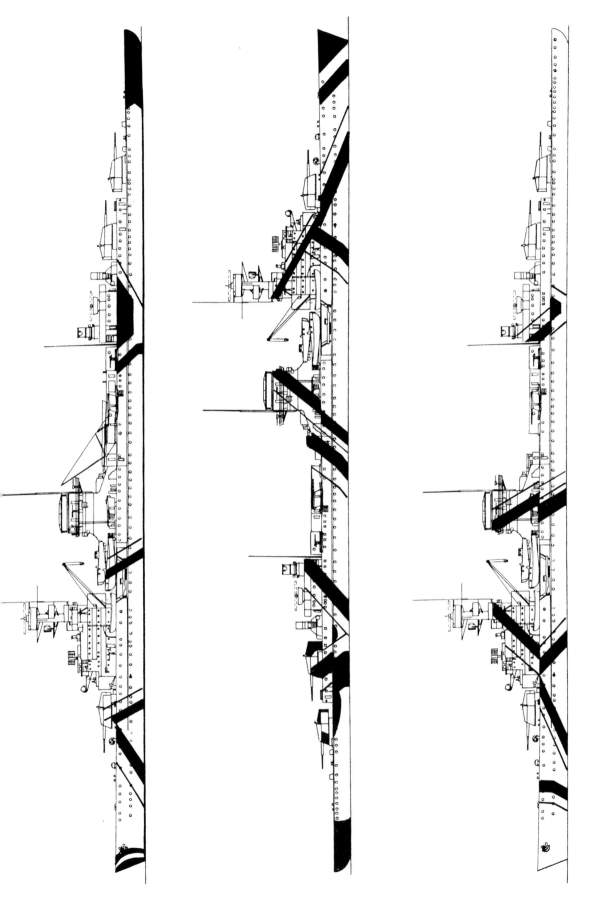

Above: *Nürnberg:* top, camouflage scheme, spring 1941; centre, 1941–42 (starboard); bottom, 1941–42 (port).

Above: *Nürnberg:* top, camouflage scheme, 1943 (starboard); bottom, camouflage scheme, 1943 (port).

Emden

The contract for Light Cruiser 'A' (Replacement *Ariadne*)— the first major warship built by Germany after the First World War—was placed at the Marinewerft, Wilhelmshaven, on 7 April 1921, the hull being launched as *Emden* on 7 January 1925. The name had been strongly advocated by *Admiral* Lorey, Director of the Museum für Meereskunde in Berlin. The baptismal speech was delivered by the Chief of Naval Staff, *Admiral* Zenker, and the widow of *Fregattenkapitän* Müller, commander of the light cruiser *Emden* sunk in 1914, named the ship. Despite the cold and heavy rain there was the usual enormous turn-out for a warship launching. Government ministers and many other dignitaries attended. The honour guard marched through Dockyard Gate 1 at 1030 past the paraded future ship's company. On the stroke of eleven the cruiser's hull trundled down to the water mounted on a keel sledge.

Emden was commissioned by *Kapitän zur See* Förster on 15 October 1925 and the usual acceptance programme was carried out by dockyard specialists and the warship testing branch. The first trials were run in the North Sea, others in the Baltic from Kiel and Pillau. In engine trials the cruiser made 29.1kt at 45,900shp; the top speed recorded was 29.4kt. During trials it became evident that the gunnery control position in the unusual tulip-shaped foretop was too confined and that various other features of the original design were unsatisfactory. In her first refit, the cruiser's battlemast was shortened by 7m and a 23m long pole mast was added at the rear of the redesigned foretop. The after funnel was raised by 2m so that both funnels stood 19m above the designed waterline, and a flying bridge was fitted to connect the bridge proper with the battlemast.

At the end of January 1926 *Emden* participated in exercises as flagship of the BSN (Commander North Sea Forces) and then continued working up. On 19/20 September she paid her first visit to the port of Emden, where the commander presented the town with a memorial tablet bearing the names of the *Emden* fallen. At this time it was being decided that the cruiser should engage in the role for which she had been designed, and on 14 November 1926, after

embarking an additional 102 cadets, she departed for her first major cruise, of sixteen months' duration.

Prewar Service

First cruise (full circumnavigation): Spain, Canary Islands, St Helena, Cape Town, Zanzibar, Mombasa, Indian Ocean to Saban and Padang, the Cocos Islands (where a memorial service was held in sight of the wreck of the World War I cruiser *Emden*), Java, Celebes, Japan and the Aleutians, Alaska, Seattle, Mexico, Ecuador, Peru, Chile, Cape Horn to the Falklands (where a memorial service was held for those lost aboard Von Spee's four cruisers on 8 December 1914), Argentina, Brazil, Haiti, the Azores and Wilhelmshaven, arriving on 14 March 1928. The cruise was a political success. Although other German warships, such as the old cruiser *Berlin*, were also showing the flag abroad, *Emden* was a new ship and impressions mattered, particularly in the Third World. After a refit the second foreign cruise began on 5 December 1928 under *Emden*'s second commander, *Fregattenkapitän* Arnauld de la Perière.

Second cruise (full circumnavigation): Cartagena (Spain), Naples, Greece, Suez, Aden, Mombasa, Netherlands East Indies, Australia, New Zealand, Fiji, Samoa and Hawaii, San Diego, Central America and Panama, returning to Wilhelmshaven on 13 December 1929. As *Karlsruhe* was not ready for her scheduled cruise, *Emden* took her place and left on 13 January 1930.

Third cruise: Madeira, US East Coast, New Orleans and Jamaica, returning to Wilhelmshaven on 13 May 1930 for refit. On 11 October 1930 *Fregattenkapitän* Witthoeft-Emden became the cruiser's third commander; he was a survivor of the first *Emden*, having been her Torpedo Officer. The cruiser was reassigned to the Naval Training Inspectorate and prepared for her fourth major cruise, leaving for the Far East on 1 December 1930.

Fourth cruise: Mediterranean, Suez, Ceylon, Siam, Philippines, China, Japan, Guam, Batavia, the Cocos Islands, Durban, Angola, Freetown, Canary Islands and Santander, returning to Wilhelmshaven on 2 December 1931.

On 1 January 1932 *Emden* was released from the Training Inspectorate and re-joined the Fleet where, under her fourth commander, *Fregattenkapitän* Grassmann (appointed in March), she participated in various exercises and made goodwill calls along the Baltic and Danish coasts. On 20 February 1933, in company with the new light cruiser *Leipzig*, she left Wilhelmshaven for the Atlantic, where the two ships held a gunnery exercise off the West African coast. On her return to Germany, *Emden* was decommissioned on 1 April for a major refit in which her four coal-fired boilers were converted to oil-firing. Her permanent ship's company transferred to the pocket-battleship *Deutschland*, commissioning the same day.

Emden was recommissioned by *Fregattenkapitän* Karl Dönitz on 29 September 1934, seventeen months later. The loss of coal bunkers following the changeover to all-oil-fired boilers created space which was used for accommodation and storage. The number of engine room personnel was cut by 39. Outward changes involved shortening both funnels by 2m; each was very slightly canted at the forward rim. The former mainmast had been cut to little more than a stump to carry the searchlight platforms. Outriggers were fitted either side of the after funnel to support the radio aerials, which were formerly strung in the mainmast crosstrees. The foretop staff was now 8m in height. A derrick with a deckhouse forward had been erected on the starboard side of the mainmast.

The new ship's permanent company was trained intensively in the two-month period before the next overseas voyage began on 11 November 1934.

Fifth cruise: Canary Islands, Cape Verde, South Africa, Seychelles, Ceylon, India, Mediterranean and Spain, returning to Wilhelmshaven on 14 June 1935. *Fregattenkapitän* Bachmann was appointed the cruiser's sixth commander in September 1935. *Emden* embarked on her next foreign cruise on 23 October 1935.

Sixth cruise: Bermudas, West Indies, north coast of South America, Panama, Hawaii, US West Coast, Panama, US East Coast, Canada and Spain, returning to Wilhelmshaven on 11 June 1936. *Kapitän zur See* Lohmann was appointed the cruiser's seventh commander in August 1936, and *Emden* sailed on her next foreign cruise on 10 October 1936. She had aboard 650 men, including four midshipmen and 160 cadets.

Seventh cruise: Sardinia, Varna/Black Sea, Constantinople, Suez, Port Said, Ceylon, Singapore, Bangkok, Borneo, Japan, China, Sumatra, East Indies, Egypt and then Spain, returning to Wilhelmshaven on 23 April 1937. *Fregattenkapitän* Bürkner assumed command in July 1937. The next voyage began in November 1937.

Eighth cruise: Indian Ocean area. The seventh and eighth voyages had been planned for longer but were curtailed for two reasons. Abroad, hostility to the German regime was growing, and many visits had been cancelled by host states. The original causes of resentment against Germany were the 1935 Nuremberg race laws, which the 1936 Berlin Olympiad had done little to mitigate, and the other was the Spanish Civil War, where German warships patrolled coastal waters as part of an international non-intervention commission. Whilst returning from the short Indian Ocean voyage, the situation had become sufficiently tense for *Emden* to be placed under the orders of the BdP (*Befehlshaber der Panzerschiffe*, Commanding Admiral Pocket-Battleships) in the Mediterranean. She patrolled off various Spanish ports and did not complete the cruise until 23 April 1938. A ninth voyage, to the United States, was eventually cancelled following adverse foreign reaction to incidents culminating in *Kristallnacht*. In June 1938 *Kapitän zur See* Wever became the cruiser's ninth commander.

Ninth cruise: *Emden* sailed for the Mediterranean on 26 July 1938, returning to Wilhelmshaven on 10 October. She sailed again in early November, lay from 12 to 18 November at Varna, Bulgaria, for the dedication of the memorial to fourteen crew members of *UB 45*, lost when the submarine was mined while leaving the port on 6 November 1916; King Boris of Bulgaria visited the ship. On 19 November *Emden* proceeded to Istanbul, where the crew took part in the state funeral for the Turkish State President Kemal Attatürk. The cruiser returned to Wilhelmshaven on 15 December 1938.

In various refits since 1936 the mainmast stump had acquired an 11m tall pole, while the radio aerial outriggers on the after funnel had been discarded in favour of a mast with struts and gaff. A third 8.8cm flak gun had been added, the three weapons being grouped in a triangular formation on the boat deck. In mid-1938 the sickle-shaped stem was replaced by a straight, slightly raked version.

World War II

In May 1939 *Kapitän zur See* Lange was appointed the cruiser's tenth commander. On the outbreak of war on 1 September 1939 *Emden* was transferred from the Training Inspectorate to the BdA (*Befehlshaber der Aufklärungsstreitkräfte*, Commanding Admiral Naval Scouting Forces), *Vizeadmiral* Densch, who aboard his flagship *Nürnberg* led a large task force consisting of the light cruisers *Königsberg*, *Leipzig* and *Köln* and numerous destroyers, minelayers and smaller craft. His mission was to extend the *Westwall* (or Siegfried Line) by mining the German

Bight seawards from the Dutch coast to the Skagerrak. The original intention of the *Westwall* was to guarantee to Hitler's neighbours to his west that he had no territorial ambitions in that direction. The operation lasted from 3 to 20 September. The German force was based at Wilhelmshaven, where it returned regularly to resupply and ship mines. On the afternoon of 4 September ten Blenheim bombers of Nos 107 and 110 Squadrons RAF approached the Jade estuary with orders to attack German warships found in the roadstead or harbour. The aircraft divided into two formations of five. Three of the five aircraft of No 107 Squadron were shot down by flak over Wilhelmshaven and a fourth crashed between the quay wall and the foredeck of *Emden* (which was berthing in the main harbour), killing nine of the cruiser's crew and injuring twenty.

During repair work a degaussing system was fitted, the cabling of which ran along the upper side of the belt armour above the waterline. The cruiser's flak was also being increased continually, 3.7cm single-mounted weapons and numerous 2cm guns, some the quadruple *Vierling*, being installed. Training duties then resumed over the winter of 1939.

On 12 March, together with the heavy cruiser *Lützow* and the oiler *Nordmark*, *Emden* put into the frozen port of Swinemünde, where she was urgently needed in support of Operation 'Weserübung', the occupation of Norway.* Group 5 for Oslo consisted of the new—and not fully worked-up—heavy cruiser *Blücher*, the flagship of *Vizeadmiral* Kummetz, *Lützow*, *Emden*, the torpedo-boats *Möwe*, *Albatros* and *Kondor*, the motor minesweepers *R 17* to *R 24* inclusive and the whalecatchers *Rau 7* and *Rau 8*. During the night of 5 April *Emden* carried out searchlight exercises with *Blücher* and the following evening embarked her 610 occupation troops with munitions and equipment at Swinemünde. *Blücher* and *Emden* left with the three torpedo-boats at 0600 on 7 April, and once at sea the crew was informed of the impending operation. On the 8th *Lützow* joined the group, taking station astern of *Blücher*, the force then steering north through the Great Belt for Oslo Fjord.

At midnight the German ships passed the entrance to Oslo Fjord, but the element of surprise had been lost. Soon the Norwegians began to douse all coastal lights and beacons, patrol vessels to port and starboard began to Morse enquiries, and warning shots were fired from the batteries at Rauöy and Bolärne. It was misty and visibility was poor. Kummetz took the questionable decision to pass the dangerous Dröbak Narrows at first light at half-ahead. At 0525 *Blücher*, the leading ship, was hit by 28cm shells, set on fire and disabled.† Upon seeing the initial attack on *Blücher* and as his own ship had received three 15cm hits and was being raked by light weapons fire, *Kapitän zur See* Thiele, *Lützow*'s commander, assumed control of the group and withdrew the force at maximum speed astern, since forcing the Narrows seemed impossible. After a reconnaissance, the invasion troops aboard *Lützow* and *Emden* were disembarked downfjord at Sonsbukten for a land assault on the Dröbak defences. After a number of *Luftwaffe* attacks, *Lützow* and *Emden* took up covering fire positions at 1555 while two torpedo-boats and four R-boats went close inshore to land naval infantry to take the Dröbak batteries, which eventually gave up without a fight.

Surrender negotiations along the fjord lasted well into the late evening, and it was not until 0845 on 10 April that *Lützow*, *Emden*, *Möwe* and the R-boats passed at speed through the Kaholm Narrows to make fast in Oslo three hours later. *Emden* was then used as a wireless communications and liaison centre between the three branches of service at Oslo, returning to Gotenhafen in the Baltic as part of the BdA force once the Norwegian situation had been consolidated in the summer. In August 1940 *Kapitän zur See* Mirow became the cruiser's eleventh commander.

The surviving light cruisers—*Nürnberg*, *Leipzig*, *Köln* and *Emden*—were all relegated by OKM to training status with effect from 7 February 1941 and did not return to battle-readiness until September that year. After the invasion of the Soviet Union the possibility was appreciated that the Russian Fleet might attempt to break out from

---

* Germany depended on supplies of Scandinavian iron ore imported in her freighters loading at Narvik. It was the legitimate practice of these ships to make their way southwards through Norwegian coastal waters so as to afford themselves immunity from attack under international law. Following earlier incidents involving the prize *City of Flint* and the oiler *Westerwald*, the storming of *Altmark* by British destroyers at Jössing Fjord on 16 February 1940 was the last straw. In the subsequent diplomatic exchanges, Norway had condemned the British action as illegal. However, as Norway had instructed her warships at the time to observe the incident and not interfere, thus failing to act as required under international law, Hitler decided that Norway would not protect his iron ore freighters either when the first incidents occurred. Thus invasion was essential.—G.B.

† Her rudder machinery failed. She had to be anchored to avoid drifting on the rocks and was then torpedoed by the shore batteries on Kaholm. The resulting fires were uncontrollable and after a magazine exploded amidships she was abandoned, sinking at 0732.

Kronstadt to internment in Sweden, and for this reason the so-called German 'Baltic Fleet', consisting of the battleship *Tirpitz*, the pocket-battleship *Admiral Scheer*, the four light cruisers and numerous smaller warships, was assembled under *Vizeadmiral* Ciliax. Once it was clear that the Russians did not have this intention, the Baltic Fleet was divided into two parts, *Emden* and *Leipzig* forming Group South based on Libau, where they remained at readiness to support the German advance through the Baltic States. Between 25 and 27 September the two cruisers gave covering fire to assist German troop landings on the Estonian island of Ösel, bombarding Russian artillery positions on the Sworbe peninsula. The two cruisers avoided torpedo attacks by Russian MTBs and a submarine.*

In November 1941, when the Fleet Training Squadron was formed, *Emden* returned to training duties. Conditions resembled peacetime, for in the Baltic Germany had control of air and sea. Between June 1942 (*Kapitän zur See* Schmidt took command of the cruiser in July 1942) and November *Emden* underwent a major refit at Wilhelmshaven. In place of the lower searchlight on the battlemast an FuMB radar mattress was installed on a slightly enlarged platform. On 7 November, in the presence of *Grossadmiral* Raeder, *Emden* became the first warship to pass through Entrance IV ('Raeder Lock') at its ceremonial opening. She remains today the largest warship ever to have passed though the lock chamber.

Although the ship achieved 26.9kt in engine trials off Neukrug, a major engine overhaul was indicated, for she had been in service for almost sixteen years and despite the changeover from coal- to oil-firing retained her original engines. Nevertheless, the financial and military situation made the postponement of a machinery refit inevitable. In September 1943 *Kapitän zur See* Henigst was appointed her thirteenth commander, relinquishing to *Fregattenkapitän* Meisner in March 1944.

On 19 September 1944, as flagship of C-in-C Minelayers operating out of Horten, Norway, *Emden* helped lay Skagerrak Minefield XXXW 'Klaudius'. On 1 October, in company with the destroyers *Karl Galster*, *Richard Beitzen*, *Friedrich Ihn* and *Z 30*, *Emden* laid Skagerrak Minefield XXXIIb 'Caligula', the group being under constant air attack during which a torpedo passed below a destroyer amidships. On 5 October the same group laid Skagerrak Minefield XXXIIa 'Vespasia'. The mines were shipped aboard the destroyers at Frederikshavn and shared out amongst the various units at Horten. The cruiser *Köln* arrived on 14 October 1944 with 90 mines shipped at Swinemünde for the 'Augustus' field, but the programme was now abandoned because of increasing enemy air raids.

Until the end of the year *Emden* ran various troopship and convoy escorts in Oslo Fjord. On 10 December she ran aground and was holed in compartment II, and this damage, combined with the general condition of her machinery, led to repairs at Schichau Werft, Königsberg. However, work proceeded at a very slow tempo. On 23 January 1945, when Russian troops closed around the city, OKM ordered the ship to be prepared to sail, and after the coffins of *Feldmarschall* von Hindenburg and his spouse had been disinterred and brought aboard the cruiser, *Kapitän zur See* Kähler, the ship's fifteenth and last commander, appointed in January, headed for Pillau with tug assistance at 0300 on the 25th. After unloading the coffins and undergoing further makeshift repairs, *Emden* took aboard her quota of refugees and wounded and sailed for Kiel on one shaft on 1 February, arriving safely after a six-day voyage at the mercy of Soviet submarines and aircraft.

In the Deutsche Werke shipyard at Kiel *Emden* was subjected to continuing air raids. On 11 March the forward deck housing and port torpedo tube set were damaged by incendiaries. On 3 April the forward funnel was destroyed by a direct hit. On 9 April, when British aircraft dropped 2,634 tonnes of bombs on Kiel, the heavy cruisers *Admiral Scheer* and *Admiral Hipper* were wrecked. A near miss astern damaged *Emden*'s stem with splinters. During the night of 13 April *Emden* was seriously damaged in an air raid, and she was towed next morning to Heikendorf Bay with a 15-degree list to port. Once the hull had been sealed, the cruiser was grounded in the shallows and deconimissioned on 26 April. On 3 May 1945 she was scuttled with explosives. Over the next five years the wreck was broken up *in situ* and scrapped.

---

* The Sworbe peninsula projects south from the Estonian Baltic island of Ösel at the mouth of the Gulf of Riga. It had been occupied by a garrison of 4,000 Russian troops since June 1940. In order to dislodge them, the Germans launched Operation 'Weststurm'. The 162nd Infantry Regiment encountered heavy resistance on 22 September 1941 and artillery support was requested from seawards. *Leipzig*, *Emden*, torpedo-boats and minesweepers bombarded Russian land installations in the Salmi-Meldri sector from Lyu Bay on the 25th and 27th of the month. On the 27th, during its withdrawal, the force was attacked without success by four Russian torpedo-cutters, one of the latter being hit and sunk by friendly fire. The submarine *SC-317* missed *Leipzig* with two torpedoes.—G.B.

Above: The light cruiser *Emden* (i), displacing 3,664 tons, was launched at Kaiserliche Werft, Danzig, on 26 May 1908 and entered service on 10 July 1909. On 17 September 1910 she arrived at the German colony of Tsingtao, China, on attachment to the German Far East Cruiser Squadron. *Korvettenkapitän* Karl von Müllier assumed command in May 1913. She was the most famous and second most successful of the German regular warship raiders of the Great War. Putting to sea from Tsingtao on 31 July 1914, she took Germany's first merchant prize on 4 August. Subsequently she ranged the oceans from the Marianas to the Maldives, sinking or capturing fifteen merchant vessels of 66,023grt. She also accounted for one Russian cruiser and a French torpedo-boat. On 9 November her presence was reported by the shore station on Direction Island and the more powerful Australian light cruiser *Sydney* was detached from a nearby troop convoy to investigate. A two-hour long battle ensued, during which *Emden* was badly damaged. His ship afire and in danger of sinking, her commander had little choice but to run her aground on North Keeling Island. As was the German naval tradition of the time, von Müller refused to strike his flag despite being unable to continue the engagement, and this caused more casualties than would otherwise have been the case. *Emden*'s dead numbered 129 naval personnel and five civilians, including three Chinese. The cruiser received the Iron Cross and upon all her crew was bestowed the unique honour of adding to their surnames '-Emden'. The last known survivor of *Emden*, engine-room Petty Officer Heyo Aden-Emden, was present at the launch of the frigate *Emden* on 17 December 1980 at the Bremer Vulkan Yard. Armament: Ten 10.5cm and eight 5.2cm guns, two torpedo tubes. Dimensions: 118.3 × 13.5 × 5.5m. Machinery: Two 3-cylinder triple-expansion steam engines supplied by twelve coal-fired boilers providing a top speed of 24kt. Crew: 18 officers and 343 men.

Below: *Emden* (ii) was launched on 1 February 1916 at AG Weser, Bremen, and entered service on 16 December 1916. As flagship of the North Sea torpedo-boat flotillas, she took part in the German troop landings on the eastern Baltic islands between 12 and 23 October and gave covering fire at Ösel and Dagö. After hostilities she arrived with the High Seas Fleet at Scapa Flow on 29 November 1918. Her crew attempted to scuttle the cruiser there on 21 June the following year, but the British succeeded in getting her into shallow water. In 1922 *Emden* (ii) was awarded to France; she was scrapped at Caen in 1926. Armament: Eight 15cm and two 8.8cm guns, four torpedo tubes. Dimensions: 151.4 × 14.3 × 6.3m (max). Machinery: Two turbines driven by twelve Schulz watertube boilers producing 31,000shp for 27.7kt. The photograph shows *Emden* (ii) in November 1918 at Wilhelmshaven prior to internment; note the disposition of the foward 15cm guns, and that she has a slimmer, more elegant hull form as compared to *Emden* (i). A characteristic of these new light cruisers was their raised forefunnel. The two 8.8cm guns were located between the mainmast and the after funnel.

Left, upper: *Emden* in the early stages of construction at the Reichsmarine Werft, Wilhelmshaven.

Left, lower: *Emden* shortly before her launch on 7 January 1925. Despite the strong breeze and rain there is a huge crowd to watch the ceremony. Lining the foredeck rail, dockyard men stand ready to let fall the anchors as soon as the hull is afloat so as to impede her progress across the basin. Just above the water can be seen the stabiliser keel; later units were fitted additionally with an anti-roll device in the form of extendible floats. At the head of the two temporary masts flies the ensign of the *Reichsmarine*, a black/white/red horizontal tricolour with a black Iron Cross at its centre.

Right, upper: At the commissioning quay, Wilhelmshaven. On the quarterdeck the crew is paraded and an honour guard presents arms as the ensign is raised to signal that *Emden* has entered service. The tall rail stanchions are for the canvas sun awning aft. Astern of *Emden* is a partly submerged floating dock, behind which is Drydock VI.

Right, lower: *Emden*'s bows. The *Reichsmarine* ensign flies at the jack. The taut stays are for the forward canvas sun awning. At the forepeak is the symbolic Iron Cross awarded to the first cruiser of the name and engraved in the same manner as all awarded during the Great War: above, the Imperial Crown; at the centre, the letter 'W' for Kaiser Wilhelm II; and below, the year of award, 1914. The Iron Cross was introduced during the Wars of Liberation in 1813. The heraldic device is the coat-of-arms of the town of Emden.

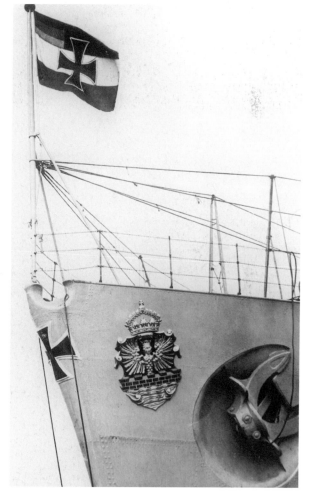

Left: The ship's bell—probably the first of the three—was a copy of that carried aboard the World War I cruiser *Emden*, cast and donated by the Marineverein Prinz Adalbert. The first bell cracked and was replaced by a bronze copy. This was melted down in 1942, an iron version being substituted which now hangs in the Senate Hall of the Marineunter-stiltzungkommando at Wilhelmshaven.

Below: The view from the battlemast over the bridge deck. On the foredeck, just visible abaft the water deflectors, is a part of the leading 15cm gun and and superfiring 'B' gunhouse. In the foreground is the command position with rangefinder, with periscope beads projecting above the roof.

Above: *Emden* as originally completed, during machinery trials on 12 January 1926. The slim, tubular foremast with its tulip-headed foretop was unique. The main gunnery control station with rangefinder was located there and was found to be unacceptably cramped. A number of other features were found unsatisfactory, leading to a refit prior to the cruiser undertaking her first overseas voyage.

Below: *Emden* after this first refit: notice the shorter battlemast with different foretop and tall pole mast; the after funnel raised to height of the forefunnel; and the flying bridge between the battlemast and the bridge deck. At the base of the battlemast is one of the two double-banked sets of torpedo tubes. On the main deck between the after funnel and the mainmast, a 15cm gun occupies the position intended originally for the second torpedo tube mounting. The raised position between the funnels is a charthouse for cadet training. There was a close affinity between *Emden* and the World War I cruiser *Karlsruhe*: *Emden*'s design was based on the blueprints for this vessel because the Ship Testing Institute, whose work was indispensable to naval architects, had been closed down after the war.

Above: This photograph clearly shows the arrangement of the two after 15cm guns. Outboard of the aftermost is the folding propeller guard. The cruiser lies alongside the Blücherbrücke at Kiel, the usual anchorage for training ships. Towering above her bow are the masts of the ill-fated sail training ship *Niobe*, lost with many cadets in a freak squall in the Baltic in 1932.

Below: A starboard view of *Emden* at anchor, her naval ensign set at the ensign staff and jack.

Above: Preparations for an overseas cruise. Alongside the cruiser is the *Langer Heinrich* floating crane, the largest in the German Navy; this has survived two world wars and is still in service at Bremerhaven. In the background (left) is the old battleship *Zähringen*, converted for use as a gunnery target.

Below: *Emden*, watched by well-wishers, about to enter the lock chamber prior to leaving on her second circumnavigation, 5 December 1928. Off her bow is the old battleship *Schlesien*, flying the flag of a *Konteradmiral* at her foretop.

Left, upper: After *Emden* had moored in the lock chamber, Fleet Commander *Vizeadmiral* Oldekop came aboard for the departure ceremony . . .

Left, lower: . . . and delivered an address to the paraded crew and cadets. Behind him is the ship's commander, *Fregattenkapitän* Arnauld de la Perière. The officer with the light-coloured greatcoat lapels is the CO Training Inspectorate, *Vizeadmiral* Förster, the cruiser's first commander.

Right, upper and lower: Each foreign cruise was attended by much official leavetaking. Here an admiral is piped aboard and receives the honour guard's 'present arms'.

Above and left: Heavy seas in Biscay and the Atlantic curling along the decks. Several crewmen have been called out to re-secure the flailing port mooring boom which has worked free.

Right, upper: *Emden* at Villagracia in northern Spain, her first port of call during her second overseas cruise. This photograph was taken on 23 December 1928 and shows the ship dressed overall and firing a salute to mark the birthday of the Queen of Spain.

Right, lower: Gunnery (left) and torpedo (right) training for crew and cadets during the cruise, with practice torpedoes retrieved by the ships' boats after release. In the photograph on the left the rangefinder of the forward fire control and the two forward gunhouses engage a target to port.

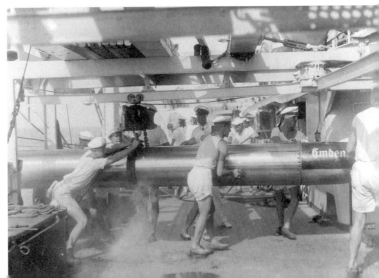

Neapel

Above: *Emden* at Naples: a view from the citadel towards Vesuvius and the Bay. The cruiser is moored stern to the breakwater.
Below: Gunnery and torpedo exercises were carried out off Argostolia, Greece, with the prewar cruiser *Berlin*. Once

Emden and the three 'K' class cruisers were in service, the old ships were gradually withdrawn. Here *Berlin* heads for Germany at the conclusion of the joint exercise.

Above: *Emden* at Constantinople. This imposing view from the German Embassy gives an impression of the size of connecting strait between the Mediterranean and Black Sea; for centuries the Russians have striven to gain possession of this strategic waterway. In the roadstead to the left of *Emden* is the ancient Turkish warship *Medjidieh*, launched in 1903 in the United States.

Below: *Emden* being coaled by native labour at Port Said, her first port of call away from the European continent. Stowage of the coal below decks and cleaning the ship afterwards was left to the crew.

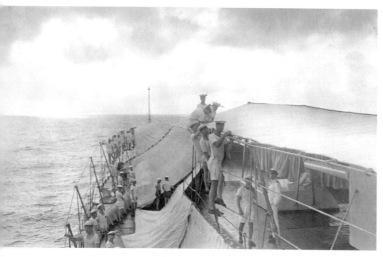

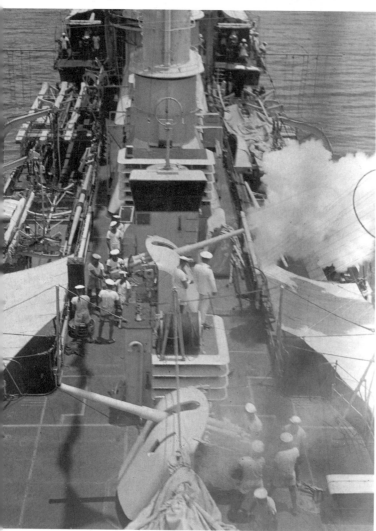

Far left, upper: Passing through the Suez Canal with awnings set. Although these made no difference to the temperature, they kept the sun off the deck, provided shade and made conditions below more tolerable.

Left, upper: A sultan is received aboard at Mombasa with full military honours. Everyone who has made a foreign voyage aboard a warship knows how much these gestures contribute to friendship and understanding.

Far left, lower: Exercising the 8.8cm flak crews. These two weapons were located between the after funnel and the mainmast. Between the two guns is a ventilator unit and abaft the funnel the radio D/F centre with loop.

Left, lower: While the ship was at Port Victoria in the Seychelles on 31 May 1929, Skagerrak Day was marked by a memorial service to the dead of the Battle of Jutland. Here the crew is assembled on the quarterdeck. The Church Parade flag flies above the national ensign at the staff.

Right: The Imperial Navy ensign is hoisted at the foretop signal yard—another tradition maintained in the *Kriegsmarine*. Viewing slits for gunnery personnel in the foretop, the rigging for the radio aerials and the two searchlight platforms are seen. On the forward face of the funnel are a vane and siren.

Below: *Emden* alongside a coaling wharf at Sabang in Sumatra. Coal was delivered aboard in hoppers on a conveyor belt— simpler and labour-saving, but not necessarily cleaner.

Above: *Emden* crew sports day at Endeh, Flores, May 1929.

Right: *Emden* in drydock at Auckland, New Zealand, for a three-day defouling and repainting in June 1929. The initial reception by the townspeople was unfriendly if not actually hostile. The excellent conduct of the crew and several favourable occurrences led to a swing to the other extreme, and many new friends had been won by the time the ship sailed.

Below: Many contacts were renewed in the former German Samoan possessions and protectorates. The cruiser is seen here anchored at Pago-Pago.

Opposite page, top: A high point was the visit to Apia, where the residents of the former German protectorate (1900–18) dispensed with formality—and so many bananas were gifted to the ship that it was a problem to know where to stow them all!

Opposite page, centre: A meeting with one of the cruisers of the US *Omaha* class in the approaches to San Diego.

Opposite page, bottom: *Emden* mooring, the manoeuvre being watched critically by her American counterparts.

Above: A stream of visitors to *Emden* at the San Diego
quayside.
Below: Well-wishers stand shoulder to shoulder to wave
Emden off on her departure, 9 September 1929.

Above: The next port of call was Panama.
Below: Entering one of the Panama Canal lock chambers to reach the Atlantic. The cruiser is already warped to one of the towing locomotives ashore.

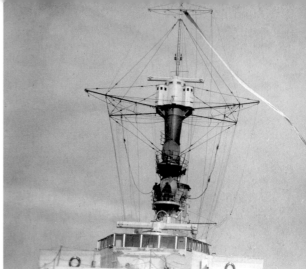

Above left: *Emden* approaching the Bay of Biscay, 11 December 1929, in the aftermath of a hurricane. The after rangefinder is well secured against the elements. The cruiser has a list, suggesting that both wind and sea are on her beam. The wave height and spindrift indicate a wind strength of Force 9–10.

Above right and right: Once *Emden* was in the English Channel, the homecoming streamer was made up and hoisted to the top pole of the battlemast.

Below: *Emden* leaving No III Lock, Wilhelmshaven, on 13 January. In the background is the *Langer Heinrich* floating crane and abeam an old battleship, probably *Schlesien*, flying the command flag of the *Befehlshaber der Linienschiffe* (CinC Battleships).

Above: For the third cruise, the cruiser's first call—as so often before and subsequently—was Funchal, Madeira. Here the commander's pinnace sets off for the quay.
Below left: A British admiral is piped aboard by a boatswain's mate and receives the salute of the commander. Behind *Kapitän zur See* de la Perière is the ladder reception party (the number of men in it varied as according to the rank and status of the visitor). In the foreground the honour guard presents arms. The admiral wears the international dress uniform of frock coat, cocked hat, epaulettes, medal clasp and sabre.

Above: Stoking the coal-fired furnaces. The rating's usual headwear was the 'man-o'-war'; the side cap was not generally introduced until after the outbreak of war.

Above: *Emden* at Flensburg-Mürwik. After four overseas cruises she returned to Fleet duty for a period. The cathedral-like edifice on the hill is the naval cadets' training school.
Below: Wreathed in smoke, the white ensign is hoisted on the mainmast; on deck are crewmen in British uniform; and *Emden* is careened to port, her main guns at maximum depression. The cruiser is starring in the U-boat film *Morgenrot* (Daybreak), one of the numerous naval movies so popular between the wars.

Left: Shortly before *Emden* decommissioned for a major refit on 18 March 1933, the cruiser's first commander, *Vizeadmiral* Förster, now CO North Sea Station, presented the ship with the nameplate from the World War I raider *Emden*. Seven former crewmen living in Wilhelmshaven attended the ceremony. Behind Förster is *Fregattenkapitän* Grassmann, commander at decommissioning. Notice the Imperial Navy ensign which covered the plaque; it was retained aboard. Other honours besides the Iron Cross at the forepeak and the nameplate were plaques inscribed 'Indian Ocean', 'Penang', 'Cocos Islands' and 'Ösel', affixed to the face of the bridge structure.

Below: The cruiser towards the end of her 1933–34 refit, undergoing boiler trials. Above her is the boom of *Langer Heinrich*.

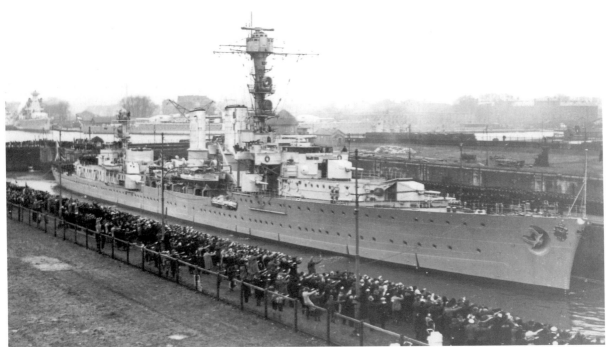

Left, upper: *Emden* re-enters service, 29 September 1934, her crew paraded aft and officers and honour guard (with weapons at 'present' during the flag-raising) on the superstructure deck. The commander stands on a raised podium. The waterline belt armour is forward of the extended propeller guard. The cruiser's nameplate can be seen above the third scuttle. On the counter at the stern is the eagle and wreathed swastika emblem—all vessels below light cruiser size carried this on the bridge face—but on the outbreak of war all heraldic shields and emblems were unshipped. It was the usual practice in the German Navy that warships undergoing extensive refit were decommissioned, in most cases the ship's company being remustered aboard another unit entering service, usually the same day.

Left, lower: *Emden* in No III Lock chamber prior to departure on 10 November 1934; the quayside is thick with well-wishers. On the opposite side of the harbour can be seen the pocket-battleships *Admiral Scheer* and *Admiral Graf Spee*.
Above: *Emden* receiving a send-off in No III Lock entrance at the start of her voyage; off-watch men wave back. On the opposite quay is the light cruiser *Leipzig* with paraded crew. On *Emden*, notice the stump mainmast (which now served only as a searchlight post), the new derrick and raised housing and the shorter funnels. The emission of black smoke has been much reduced since the changeover to oil-firing.

71

Above: *Emden* at Cape Town for a midsummer Christmas and
New Year 1934, with awnings erected. Receptions were
always held on the quarterdeck.
Below: *Emden* passing through the Kiel Canal. The old steam
pinnace with white funnel suggests that the photograph was
taken from one of the pre-dreadnought battleships, *Schlesien*
or *Schleswig-Holstein*.

Above left: The sixth overseas cruise to the Americas and Hawaii lasted from 23 October 1935 to 11 June 1936. Here the Governor of the Azores is received aboard with full ceremony at the first port of call, Angra do Heroismo.

Above right: On 7 November 1935, during the cruise, the crew was mustered on the quarterdeck to be read an Order of the Day signed by Hitler. An honour guard was present to mark a change of naval ensign—the introduction of the *Reich* War Flag aboard ship. The Order read: 'Soldiers of the *Wehrmacht*. With effect from today I present to the reconstituted *Wehrmacht* for general service use the new *Reich* War Flag. The swastika is the symbol of unity and purity of the nation, an image of the National Socialist world view, the pledge of freedom and strength of the *Reich*. The Iron Cross is to remind you of the unique traditions of our armed forces, whose virtues and example inspire you. The *Reich* colours—black, white and red—bind you to loyal service unto death. It is your pride to serve the colours. The former *Reich* War Flag will be honourably withdrawn. I reserve to myself the right to order it flown on certain memorial days.'

Below: *Emden* being towed into a lock chamber by one of the typical Panama Canal locomotives during a transit in December 1935.

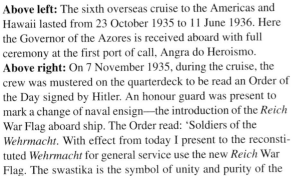

Left, upper: As always when overseas, the commander—as were all visitors of rank—was afforded a degree of ceremony depending on status when boarding or disembarking the ship. The captain was entitled to an honour guard with drummer; an admiral merited a trumpeter too, plus boatswain's whistle and a ladder reception party. Following *Kapitän zur See* Bachmann is his ADC, wearing aiguillettes.

Left, lower: During early January 1936 *Emden* called at San José, Guatemala. The crew, including brass band, travelled by train to the capital for certain national festivities. Here *Kapitän zur See* Bachmann takes the salute together with various dignitaries.

Above: *Emden* at Montreal between 12 and 18 May 1936. Notice the *Reich* national flag at the jack: this flag was flown at the ensign staff by German merchant vessels.

Right: *Emden* at Port-au-Prince flying the *Reich* War Flag and White Ensign at half mast, to observe, on Hitler's order, the passing of the British hero of Jutland, Admiral of the Fleet John Jellicoe, on 20 November 1935. The burial took place on the 25th.

Top: *Emden* on her return to Germany on 11–12 June 1936, passing *Karlsruhe* bound for Kiel and extensive repairs. Both cruisers have their crews paraded at the ships' rail.

Right: As always for overseas cruises, there was a big send-off. The two admirals are the CinC North Sea Station (IIAdN) and the Head of the Training Inspectorate. The officer at the far left, wearing aiguillettes, is an Admiral's ADC. This is winter uniform: the white-crowned cap was worn from 20 April to 30 September.

Below, left and right: An *Emden* crewman has died far from home. The coffin is placed on the quarterdeck with an honour guard—here a cadet and a rating—bearing a side-arm in the right hand. After the religious service the body is committed to the deep in keeping with naval tradition.

Right, upper: The last overseas cruise was to the Mediterranean. Between 12 and 18 November 1938 at Varna, Bulgaria, *Emden* took part in a ceremony dedicating a memorial to the casualties of *U 45*, sunk in the Black Sea in 1916. Wearing the raincoat is King Boris of Bulgaria during a shipboard visit; behind him, wearing a white belt, is his naval ADC.

Right, lower: The officer corps of the cruiser in formal dress—frock coat, cocked hat, epaulettes, medal clasp and sabre. The epaulette tassels were worn by the ranks of *Oberleutnant zur See* and above. The officer seventh from the right is a naval official and wears a naval cap with silver insignia and silver cord chinstrap; naval officers wore gold lace and insignia. Tenth from the right is *Kapitän zur See* Lohmann, commander of *Emden* from 1936 to 1938.

Below: *Emden* in 1937–38 with her new bow form.

Above: *Emden* (left) at war in the wake of light cruiser *Königsberg* during BdA exercises in the Baltic between 1 and 3 November 1939.

Below: *Emden* in the Baltic, probably in 1941.

Right, upper: The ship photographed in the Norwegian skerries the 1940–41. The radar unit has not yet been installed, and the cruiser wears the camouflage pattern in force for all warships operational in the Baltic area until 1942. The dazzle scheme used from 1942 until the war's end was a dark iron grey with stern and bow sections in light grey to deceive enemy observers as to the ship's length.

Right, lower: The wreck of *Emden* at Kiel, photographed between 3 and 14 April 1945. The ship is partially covered by camouflage netting, but the scale of the destruction is nevertheless obvious—large holes forward, heavy damage amidships and the forefunnel knocked away. The ship was towed into Heikendorf Bay, grounded and scuttled with explosives on 3 May 1945.

Königsberg

The building contract for Light Cruiser 'B' (Replacement *Thetis*) was placed with Marinewerft, Wilhelmshaven, in 1925 under Yard Number 108. The first keel material was laid on 12 April 1926 and the hull was launched on 26 March 1927 as *Königsberg*. The *Bürgermeister* of Königsberg delivered the baptismal speech, and *Frau* Loof, widow of the commander of the earlier cruiser *Königsberg*, performed the naming ceremony.

On 17 April 1929 *Fregattenkapitän* Wolf von Trotha commissioned *Königsberg* into the *Reichsmarine*, the ship's company transferring aboard from the cruiser *Nymphe*, which had decommissioned the previous day. After the usual trials and working-up, *Königsberg* represented the German *Reich* at the Barcelona World Exhibition between 18 and 26 October under a new commander, *Fregattenkapitän* Robert Witthöft-Emden (appointed in June), and she joined the Fleet on 17 December 1929.

Prewar Service

On 1 January 1930 the office of BdA (*Befehlshaber der Aufklärungsstreitkräfte*, Commanding Officer Naval Scouting Forces) was created and *Königsberg* took her place as flagship of a group consisting of *Köln*, several torpedo-boat flotillas and a minesweeping half-flotilla. Between 2 April and 19 June, as flagship of *Vizeadmiral* Gladisch, BdA, and in company with other German warships, she paid a goodwill visit to Spain and the Mediterranean. Calls were made at Vigo, Almeria, Catania, Argostolion, Split, Port Mahon and Lisbon.

In September 1930 *Fregattenkapitän* Hermann Densch was appointed the cruiser's third commander. Structural changes to the ship during the year included the placing of a platform forward of the battlemast at the level of the lower bridge deck.

In a two-month refit at the beginning of 1931, the tall pole mast at the foretop was shortened, although the long signal yards were retained. The after deckhouse was given a single-storey extension at its forward end. On 19 May that year *Königsberg* took part in the Fleet celebrations before *Reich* President Hindenburg on the occasion of the launching of the pocket-battleship *Deutschland* at

Kiel. During a summer cruise, with manoeuvres between 15 June and 3 July, various Norwegian fjords were visited. In early August the cruiser participated in competitive exercises at Kiel before 'showing the flag' off the Baltic resort of Scharbeutz on 15–16 August.

During a refit the following winter the extension to the after deckhouse was enlarged forward by one deck with a gallery. In addition to the usual exercises and visits along the German coast, between 11 and 17 June *Königsberg* visited Stockholm in company with five torpedo-boats. *Fregattenkapitän* Otto von Schrader became the cruiser's fourth commander in September.

The 1933 New Year naval parade was broadcast from aboard *Königsberg*. The cruiser formed part of the review honouring the visit of Hitler to Kiel on 22–23 May. In company with the old battleship *Schleswig-Holstein*, she visited the Norwegian fjords between 26 July and 6 August. From 14 to 18 August she took part in the Fleet torpedo exercises with *Schleswig-Holstein*, *Schlesien* and *Hessen*, the light cruiser *Leipzig*, torpedo-boats and minesweepers.

In a 1934 refit the port crane and gear were replaced by a bar crane, and two 8.8cm single flak guns installed on the roof of the after deckhouse. The platform erected in 1930 was landed and the platform on the lower bridge deck enlarged instead. The bridge deck was lengthened as far back as the forefunnel. On 9 July, as flagship of *Konteradmiral* Kolbe, BdA, *Königsberg* met *Leipzig* in the Jade and made the first German naval goodwill visit to Britain since the Great War, mooring at Portsmouth from the 11th to 15th of the month and returning to Kiel on the 20th via the Irish Sea and Fair Isle. Later in July that year the cruiser called at Reval and the Estonian islands before taking part in the autumn Fleet Manoeuvres. *Fregattenkapitän* Hubert Schmundt was appointed her fifth commander in September.

An aircraft catapult was fitted during a dockyard lay-up early in 1935. At the beginning of February the ship made a round voyage from Wilhelmshaven to Bremen via the Channel and the north of Scotland. *Königsberg* took part in Navy Week at Kiel in June and in the Fleet gunnery exercises on 19 August in the presence of Hitler aboard the state yacht *Grille*. The Polish port of Gotenhafen was visited from 22 to 25 August. A full schedule of exercises occupied the remainder of the year.

In a 1936 winter refit the aerial booms on the after funnel were replaced by a pole mast with crosstrees. The after deckhouse was converted and enlarged so that the rangefinder could be sited further aft, and a raised flak fire control centre was erected forward of the deckhouse. A light pole mast was set at the forward wall of this structure, slightly off-centre to starboard, while 8.8cm twin mountings replaced the single-mounted flak.

On 23 February 1936 *Königsberg*'s function as the BdA flagship was terminated and the cruiser was redesignated Gunnery Inspectorate Training Ship. The first gunnery classes were embarked on 3 March. As a result of the outbreak of civil war in Spain in July, the German government sent warships to the peninsula for the protection and evacuation of German citizens there. On 25 November *Königsberg* left Kiel and three days later relieved *Köln* at El Ferrol, commencing anti-contraband patrols off Cadiz. A call was made at Melilla. The cruiser spent Christmas at Lagos in Portugal and on 26 December intervened to release the German steamer *Palos*, which had been seized by Red Spanish forces. As a reprisal, the Red steamer *Maria Junquera* was confiscated.

On 15 January 1937 the cruiser arrived at Kiel and resumed her training role after a short overhaul. *Kapitän zur See* Robin Schall-Emden was appointed as her seventh commander in February. A visit was made to the Norwegian fjords between 12 and 28 June. The cruiser began a three-month refit on 5 December, and between 1937 and 1939 experiments were made with various radar-rangefinding devices on the roof of the bridge porch.

After the usual engine trials, training duties were resumed on 4 March 1938. *Königsberg* was at Kiel as part of the Naval Review held on 22 August in the presence of Hitler and the Hungarian regent Admiral Horthy on the occasion of the launching of the heavy cruiser *Prinz Eugen*. *Kapitän zur See* Ernst Scheurlen was appointed commander in November.

After attending the launching of the heavy cruiser *Seydlitz* at Bremen on 19 January 1939, *Königsberg* underwent a short refit and then continued as a target ship for the U-boat School. From 11 to 15 May she visited Wasa in Finland and from the 17th to 19th Visby on Gotland. *Kapitän zur See* Kurt-Caesar Hoffmann served as commander between June and September, when *Kapitän zur See* Heinrich Ruhfus was appointed her tenth and last captain.

World War II

At the outbreak of war *Königsberg* was returned to the BdA and from 3 to 20 September, in company with *Nürnberg* (flagship BdA, *Konteradmiral* Densch), *Leipzig*, *Köln*, *Emden* and numerous minelayers, destroyers and torpedo-boats, she took part in the hurried minelaying operation to extend the *Westwall* (Siegfried Line) from the Dutch coast to the north of Denmark. From 1 to 3 November, with other cruisers, *Königsberg* participated in a BdA exercise in the Baltic before re-joining *Nürnberg* and torpedo-boats of the 6th Flotilla in the German Bight, where on 12 and 13 November the group formed a reception force to escort home German destroyers returning from a minelaying operation in the Thames estuary. On 19 November she entered the yards for a refit.

In her final refit the bridge and helm position wings were shortened and reinforced and a degaussing system was installed. *Königsberg* was inactive during the winter months of 1939 on account of the severe weather. No engine trials, battle training or gunnery practice were possible, and 30 per cent of the ship's company was fresh to the cruiser when she left the yards.

At the beginning of March the first preparations were taken in hand for 'Weserübung', the invasion of Denmark and Norway. Initially *Königsberg* had been listed with Warship Group 5 (Oslo), but she changed places with the heavy cruiser *Blücher*, which was even less battle-ready. Together with sister-ship *Köln*, the gunnery training ship *Bremse*, the 1st E-Boat Flotilla with tender *Carl Peters*, the torpedo-boats *Leopard* and *Wolf* and the armed trawlers *Alteland* (*Schiff 9*) and *Koblenz* (*Schiff 18*), *Königsberg* formed Warship Group 3 with the objective of capturing the Norwegian naval base and port of Bergen. The whole operation had the highest degree of secrecy. Naval Command North Sea gave the Director of Fitting-Out, *Kapitän zur See (Ing.)* Zieb, the task of planning the necessary measures at Wilhelmshaven Navy Yard.

For embarking troops and equipment Zieb chose anchorages not overlooked from the city. These were sealed off for ease of control. Within the harbour, security was enforced by a naval artillery detachment. Transport trains were routed to dockyard tracks well outside the city and unloading bays chosen for ease of switching. Railway cranes unloaded heavy equipment and eighty electric trucks carted material to the ships. Broad gangways were put in place for the embarkation of Army personnel and sufficient cordage and wire were made available to lash down field kitchens, motor-cycles and such like. Quayside lighting was strictly controlled. On the issue of a

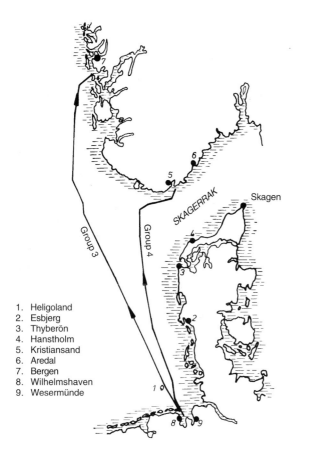

1. Heligoland
2. Esbjerg
3. Thyberön
4. Hanstholm
5. Kristiansand
6. Aredal
7. Bergen
8. Wilhelmshaven
9. Wesermünde

Above: General courses of Warship Groups 3 (Bergen) and 4 (Kristiansand), 8–9 April 1940.

specific codeword, all telephones bar two under special supervision were disconnected and all ferries bar one confined with special orders. The Kaiser Wilhelm bridge and inner lock gate were opened two hours before the first trains arrived and not shut until two hours after the ships sailed.

On 2 April *Köln*, *Königsberg* and *Bremse* occupied their appointed anchorages. On the 3rd and 4th the 8,000-ton tankers *Kattegat* and *Skagerrak* sailed for Narvik and Trondheim respectively. On the evening of 7 April the transport trains arrived in quick succession. All troops were aboard ship with their equipment by 2300, and the ships sailed at midnight. A total of 1,900 men had been embarked. Aboard *Königsberg* were *Vizeadmiral* von Schrader, Admiral-Designate Commanding Norwegian West Coast and his Staff; *Oberst Graf* von Stolberg, CO 159th Infantry Regiment, and staff; 639 men of the 69th Infantry Division; and about 100 men of the 126th Naval Artillery Detachment.

The whole plan went off smoothly and secrecy was excellent.* The group headed to sea at 18kt—the top speed of the slowest ship, *Bremse*. Once into the German Bight the crews were informed of the destination. The first *Luftwaffe* escorts appeared during the morning. Later the two torpedo-boats and *Carl Peters* joined the convoy as anti-submarine protection. Mist and decreasing visibility made progress difficult. None of the ships was equipped with radar.

During the afternoon Group West warned of light British forces between the Shetlands and Bergen. The shipboard *B-Dienst* (wireless monitoring crew) picked up radio traffic between two Royal Navy light cruisers and destroyers. Towards 1800, off Stavanger, the northbound German group passed within 60 miles of the incoming eastbound British 2nd Cruiser Squadron with eleven destroyers. At 2140 the E-boats, coming up from Heligoland, took station in the formation, and on approaching Norwegian waters all hoisted the White Ensign as a ruse to deceive Norwegian coastal forces. The Norwegians had been alerted, however, and had extinguished their coastal lights and radio beacons, leaving the German force to navigate upfjord through waters strewn with numerous small islands and rocks, many submerged at high water, without a pilot—a feat requiring great navigational skill.

Konteradmiral Schmundt ordered a reduction in speed to 7kt, the torpedo-boat *Leopard* leading, followed by the E-boats. They passed Marstein at 0200, and forty minutes later the two armed trawlers arrived to disembark from *Königsberg* the naval artillery troops who were to tackle the Kvarven torpedo batteries at the head of By Fjord directly before Bergen. The majority of the infantry were to be landed from E-boats. Their knowledge of the location and strength of Norwegian positions was vague. The force stopped and the E-boats came alongside, but the troop transfer was interrupted by an inquisitive patrol boat. The explanation was accepted, but the German ships were reported shortly afterwards by other patrol vessels. The deception succeeded to the extent that a Norwegian

---

* *Konteradmiral* Zieb remained as Senior Shipyard Director at Wilhelmshaven until 1950. He stated that shortly after the end of the war he was summoned into the presence of the Senior British Officer, Captain R. N. Condor, to witness the decoration of four dockyard workers. They were four Englishmen who had been working at the yard pre-war and continued to do so 'as Germans' throughout hostilities despite the 'perfect' security system and its police organs. When asked, all four stated that they had had no knowledge of the plans for 'Weserübung'.

torpedo-boat returned its only torpedo tube to the 'rest' position. However, it was not long before the Norwegian government ordered its coastal stations to fire on all German warships in Norwegian waters.

At 0430 the codeword 'Weserzeit' was broadcast, ordering the execution of Operation 'Weserübung' forthwith. *Köln* and *Königsberg* began transferring their troops into E-boats and ships' launches alongside, speed being of the essence, for the German force was supposed to be off Bergen at 0515. *Konteradmiral* Schmundt had decided to storm the port as the result of information that Group 5 had encountered resistance from shore batteries in Oslo Fjord.

Köln was the first to set off, and in company with *Wolf* and *Leopard* approached By Fjord. Here she was caught in the beams of a number of searchlights and bombarded by the 21cm guns of the Kvarven battery. They scored no hits and *Köln* did not reply. Once into the port of Bergen, *Köln* anchored to disembark the remainder of her troops, the two torpedo-boats following suit alongside the quay. A short while later *Bremse* and *Carl Peters* limped into harbour after running the gauntlet. *Bremse* had taken a serious hit in the stern and two hits along the waterline; her innards devastated, she had four dead and 14 wounded. *Carl Peters* had taken a hit on her mast and had dead and wounded from flying splinters amongst her Army personnel.

After her first contingent had been transferred according to plan, *Königsberg* worked up to 22kt in pursuit of the other units. At the entrance to By Fjord she was illuminated by searchlights on the Habsö bend and taken under fire at once by the 21cm batteries. She did not reply until hit, and then responded with all barrels. The first hit had penetrated the starboard side at compartment X, boring a hole 35cm in diameter immediately above the waterline at frame 107/108 and exploding in upper wall passage X.9.3. Splinters tore the bulkheads of adjacent fuel bunkers, E-plant III and boiler room II, causing substantial damage, flooding and fire in the E-room. Casualties were limited to burns cases. The shore batteries had several targets to occupy their attention, and during pauses in firing attempts were made to get a fix on the positions of the Norwegian guns from their muzzle flashes against the dark cliff. The second hit struck astern near the forward pair of 3.7cm flak guns, killing three and wounding seventeen of the gun crews. The third hit struck close to the second, passing through the afterdeck and exploding on the starboard side in the compartment XIII mess deck, gutting it completely. Later it was considered possible that the second and third

hits were the same shell which had split on striking the deck.

The visible external damage was a hole 2.5m by 0.6m on the starboard afterdeck, while the leading funnel had two holes 0.25m in diameter and E-plant IV exhaust shaft was destroyed. There was flooding below decks and the foretop had to be shut down because of smoke, fire control being transferred to the forward command position. While temporary repairs were made, the cruiser ran into Pudde Fjord at 22kt and took up station about 500m astern of *Köln*, from where she could continue firing at the Kvarven and Hellen batteries while her wounded were shipped to a dressing station ashore. Attempts to restore steam were hindered by flooding in the boiler rooms and the cruiser drifted slowly through the harbour, unable to anchor because the capstans had no electrical power. Once she succeeded in dropping anchor, her stern was caught by the tidal stream and the cruiser collided with a Swedish steamer. This happened just as the Hellen batteries began to strad-

Below: Course of Warship Group 3 (Bergen), 9 April 1940.

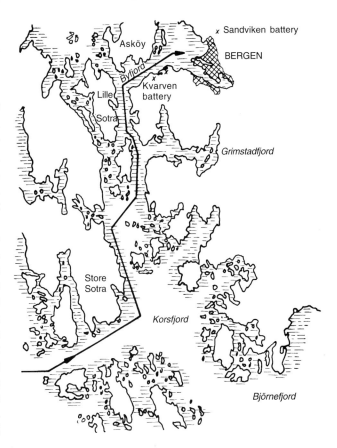

dle her with 21cm shells. This battery was silenced by full salvos from *Köln* and *Königsberg*, bombing by He 111 aircraft and finally capture by Army units.

By midday the town of Bergen, the port and surrounding defensive installations were in German hands. The 60–80 merchant vessels in the roadstead were examined by prize commandos and enemy-owned ships were impounded. At 1700 *Konteradmiral* Schmundt held a commanders' conference at which the return of warships to Germany was discussed. *Köln* and the two torpedo-boats were undamaged and would sail next evening. *Carl Peters*, the E-boats and the two armed trawlers would remain at Bergen. *Königsberg* and *Bremse* were not sufficiently seaworthy and would be detached to Admiral Commanding Norwegian West Coast as floating batteries to oppose expected British landings. Between 1430 and 1740 offshore a powerful British force was met by 47 Ju 88 and 41 He 111 bombers. Hits were obtained on the battleship *Rodney* and the cruisers *Devonshire*, *Glasgow* and *Southampton*. The destroyer *Gurkha* was sunk. Four Ju 88s were lost.

During the evening, while refuelling the torpedo-boat *Wolf* and unloading material into the aviation support ship *Bernhard von Tschierschky*, *Königsberg* came under fire from light weapons on an high point in western Pudde Fjord.

After a thorough mechanical inspection of the cruiser by the Group Engineer, *Konteradmiral* Schmundt accepted that *Königsberg* would need a further twenty-four hours at Bergen for repairs and would sail on the night of 10 April. In the late evening twelve Wellington bombers attacked *Köln* and *Königsberg*, but although bombs fell within 50m of the latter no further damage was inflicted. At nightfall beacons were lit on various high points around Bergen to mark the area in German hands and *Königsberg* moored with her starboard side against Skottegrunds Quay, thus enabling her broadside to bear on the north channel entrance to the roadstead. The E-boats were secured nearby as floating torpedo batteries. A British reconnaissance aircraft was seen but the night passed relatively quietly. About 100 crewmen were commandeered to land batteries and the railway station. The engine room personnel worked feverishly at the shipboard repairs while the remaining crew slept at their battle stations.

At 0737 on 10 April an aircraft resembling an He 111 was seen circling the harbour, and at 0800 a British attack came. Fifteen Royal Navy Skua dive-bombers from 800 and 803 Naval Air Squadrons at Hatston in the Orkney Islands, each carrying a single 100lb bomb, fell on various ships in Bergen harbour. *Königsberg* was the target for several aircraft which, after penetrating her flak, were able to place their bombs fairly precisely. The cruiser received at least three direct hits and three near misses.

Because of the speed at which the attack occurred, the sequence is not certain. The first bomb hit the quayside then penetrated ship's side at compartment VIII, exploding in the 'tween deck. The hole was so large that crew members, bodies and stretcher cases were able to pass through it directly from ship to quayside. The second bomb (which may in fact have been two) passed through the signal bridge on the port side and fell into the sea near E-plant IV, tearing a 3m^2 hole in the hull at the waterline when it exploded. The third bomb passed through the auxiliary boiler room and exploded in 'tween deck compartment VII and at the neck of the funnel. The fourth bomb hit upper deck compartment VI, passed through the Executive Officer's quarters and exploded in the 'tween deck above the auxiliary machinery room on the starboard side. The fifth bomb was a near miss which fell astern to port, although the explosion caused hull damage aft, and the sixth bomb passed through the upper deck and exploded in the 'tween deck in compartment IX.

The cruiser assumed a list to port and the order to prepare to abandon ship followed almost at once. After all rooms had been searched for personnel, the dead and wounded were brought out to the quayside followed by light weapons, flak ammunition and other valuable equipment from the upper deck. *Königsberg*'s situation at this time was very critical. Boiler room III had flooded, probably as a result of the leak plugs being blown out of place by a bomb blast. Water had also reached boiler room II, apparently by way of a damaged transverse bulkhead. This meant that all four boiler rooms were flooded to some degree. The turbine and auxiliary machinery rooms and armour deck were undamaged. Fatalities were restricted to the 'tween deck and the radio transmitting room in compartment XII. There was no electric current because the boiler rooms and electrical plant had had to be shut down and the diesel generator had not been repaired after the shell hit the previous day. This meant that a raging inferno in compartment VIII and adjacent rooms could not be put out, all attempts using hand extinguishers and other means having been found ineffective. As a damage limitation exercise the torpedo tubes were swung outboard to prevent fire reaching the warheads. The shipboard aircraft could not be flown off. Before the ship was finally abandoned all magazine doors were opened to allow flooding. Small explosions occurred amidships when fire reached the aviation spirit and ready flak ammunition.

The ship's company left the cruiser in an exemplary manner and paraded by divisions for roll call about 100m from the quayside. The air attack claimed eighteen dead and 23 injured, twelve seriously. The ship's list gradually increased and *Königsberg* turned turtle and sank with her flag flying at 1051 on 10 April 1940.

During 1941 shipyard specialists arrived from Wilhelms-haven with vessels and gear to commence salvage work. The hull was sealed, drained and, once refloated, towed by Norwegian tugs to Hagenaes Bay and anchored. The superstructure underwater was cut away and the hull righted using four winches and twenty-six 100-tonne pontoons. The wreck was scrapped over the course of the next few years.

Right, upper: The light cruiser *Königsberg*, 3,390 tons, was launched at Kaiserliche Werft, Kiel, in December 1905 and entered service on 6 April 1907. On the outbreak of war she was used as a raider and sank one ship, Ellerman's *City of Winchester* (6,601grt) and a motor lighter. On 20 September, outside Zanzibar harbour, *Königsberg* found the British cruiser *Pegasus* (2,135 tons) repairing boilers and sank her after a short action. As his own ship required an overhaul *Fregattenkapitän* Looff now entered the Rufiji Delta. Because of sandbanks at the entrance the channel was inaccessible to British cruisers on account of their greater draught, but once they had reached the delta *Königsberg* was trapped. She remained there for the next ten months, fulfilling her role of tying down a larger enemy naval force urgently required elsewhere. Three heavy-gun monitors sent from Britain joined the force and action between *Königsberg* and British naval and air units eventually began on 6 July 1915. Once she was beyond repair, the cruiser was scuttled on 11 July. Armament: Ten 10.5cm guns, ten 3.7cm automatic cannon and two torpedo tubes. Machinery: 3-cylinder triple-expansion steam engines supplied by eleven coal-fired boilers, speed 24.lkt. Dimensions: 114.8 × 13.2 × 5.2m. Peacetime complement 14 officers and 308 men. The photograph shows *Königsberg* on Fleet duty prior to 1911. Notice the heraldic shield at the forepeak; later, simpler devices were fitted either side near the bow anchor. The 3.7cm automatic cannon were located in the bow recesses and the swallow's nests behind folding screens.

Right, lower: The light cruiser *Königsberg* (ii), 5,440 tons, was launched at AG Weser Bremen on 18 December 1915 and entered service on 12 August 1916. As flagship of *Kommodore* von Reuter, II Reconniassance Group North Sea Station, the cruiser took part in the Ösel operation off Lithuania. After the Armistice in November 1918 the ship brought *Konteradmiral* Meurer to Britain for negotiations. Decommissioned on 31 May 1920, the cruiser was handed over to France as partial reparation on 20 July and entered service with the French Navy on 6 October the same year, now renamed *Metz*. She was scrapped in 1936. Armament: Eight 15cm guns, two 8.8cm flak, 4 torpedo tubes. Machinery: steam turbines driven by twelve coal-fired watertube boilers, 45,900shp, speed 27.8kt. Dimensions: 145.8 × 14.2 × 6.32m. Complement: 17 officers and 458 men (26 more as flagship). The photograph was taken in 1918 and shows the cruiser in drift ice in the Baltic.

Left: The new hull on the stocks before launching, 26 March 1927. The heraldic shield is concealed by a drape of flag-cloth. In the foreground is the baptismal pulpit. The two great anchors will arrest the progress of the ship once she is afloat.
Below: A view of the baptismal pulpit immediately before the launching.
Right, upper: The cruiser slides into her natural element. Along the rail is the canvas bearing the ship's name, on the stem at the forepeak the heraldic device.
Right, lower: In the harbour basin tugs turn the hull and bring the ship to her anchorage. This photograph was taken from a shipyard crane in the fitting-out basin at the Wilhelmshaven Navy Yard. To the right is the canal leading from the ship-building harbour into the basin.

Above: The cruiser fitting out in one of the drydocks. 'B' and 'C' 15cm turrets are already installed.

Left: *Königsberg* fitting out. On the hook of the giant *Langer Heinrich* crane is the barbette for 'A' turret. Nearer the camera is the recently launched sister-ship *Köln*.

Above: *Königsberg* approaching completion in drydock: a starboard view from forward.

Right: *Königsberg* nears completion. Between her hull and the quay is *Köln*, showing the 15cm barbette of 'A' turret and the foundations for battlemast with the forward command centre in position. In the background (left) is the old pre-dreadnought *Hannover* in front of Docks IV–VI.

Left and above: 17 April 1929: the commissioning of *Königsberg* alongside the fitting-out quay at Wilhelmshaven Navy Yard. The light cruiser *Nymphe* had decommissioned earlier, her crew transferring to the new ship. Left, the flag visible at *Nymphe*'s jackstaff indicates that the ship has been decommissioned; above, naval colours being raised at *Königsberg*'s ensign staff.

Left: Battle honours of earlier ships bearing the name were displayed prominently.

Right: The prow of the new cruiser. The device at the head of the stem was later removed and replaced by a heraldic shield mounted either side of the bow.

Below: *Königsberg*'s corps of officers and lower deck officers on the day of commissioning. The concept of 'lower deck officers' was abolished in the 1930s and replaced with a unified Warrant Officer corps.

Left, top: *Königsberg* running machinery trials over the measured mile, as indicated by the signal flags at the pole mast.

Left, centre: The cruiser heeling heavily to starboard during turning circle trials at high speed, 7 August 1929.

Left, bottom: *Königsberg* careened to port, probably for technical work on the starboard side. This sort of photograph is often explained incorrectly as an inclinometer test.

Right, upper: *Königsberg* at Stockholm in June 1932. In the foreground her accompanying torpedo-boats are moored in two packs.

Right, lower: *Königsberg* at a naval review in 1931, the pennant of the BdA (Commander Reconnaissance Forces) at the foretop. Her ensign has been retouched. Astern lie a light cruiser and a line of torpedo-boats.

Left: In July 1934 German warships made an official visit to a British port for the first time since the Great War. Here *Königsberg* (right) and *Leipzig* are seen alongside at Portsmouth.

Below: In August 1935 *Königsberg* visited the Polish port of Gotenhafen (Gdynia), where the cruiser is seen alongside the railway terminus quay.

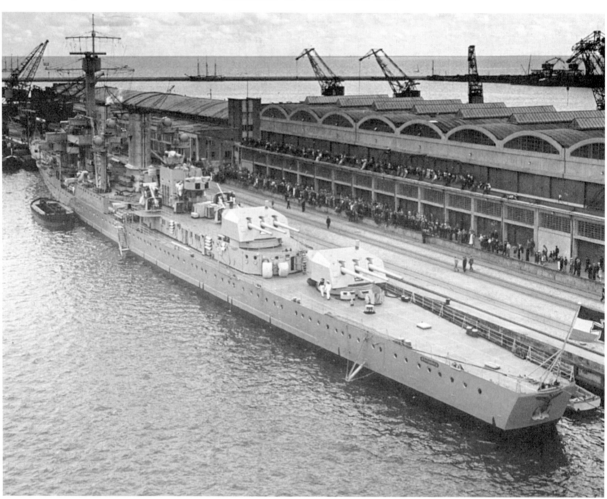

Above: *Königsberg* leaving
Wilhelmshaven No III Entrance.
Right, upper: Exercises and training: a
stern–bow refuelling manoeuvre as seen
from the torpedo-boat *Falke*.
Right, lower: A stern view of
Königsberg dressed overall.

Far left: The sunny side of naval cruises—fine weather, a smooth sea, the crew sunbathing on the foredeck. This view forward shows the 15cm barrels of 'A' turret, anchor capstans and chains.

Left, upper: *Königsberg* at her buoy at Kiel, the crew at work washing and retouching the paintwork. In the background is her sister-ship *Karlsruhe*.

Left, lower: 'A' turret firing a full salvo ahead. Note the collapsed rail stanchions and the great billow of powder smoke.

Left, bottom: A view of 'B' and 'C' turrets from astern, port side. Here the cruiser is passing through the lock; the two signalmen with flags atop the turrets suggest some form of tricky manoeuvre.

Above: Exercising the main armament to port at high speed. 'A' turret has just fired.

Right, upper: At the end of the exercise, criticism and a closing address from the Gunnery Officer.

Right, lower: Flak. Initially these were 8.8cm C/13 guns on a central pivoting chassis, later an improved model of the same calibre.

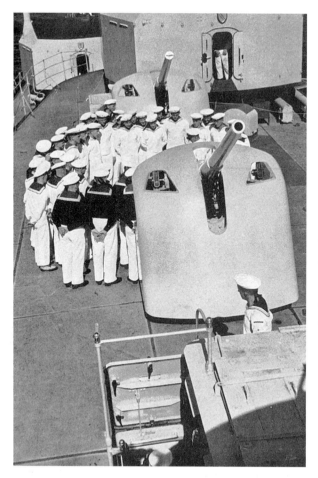

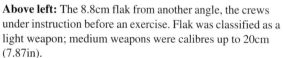

Above left: The 8.8cm flak from another angle, the crews under instruction before an exercise. Flak was classified as a light weapon; medium weapons were calibres up to 20cm (7.87in).

Above right: Emphasis was placed on night firing—one of the positive lessons of the Great War. This involved intensive searchlight training. This is a view forward to the starboard searchlight position; left alongside is the after command post housing; and at the foretop is a navigational lantern.

Below left: The engine room control centre. A command-relay rating stands with a telephone amidst numerous monitoring instruments.

Below right: The electrical control room.

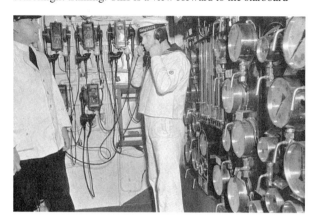

Above: From 1935, 'K' class cruisers were fitted with an aircraft catapult located between the two funnels. The photograph shows the arrangement aboard *Königsberg* with a Heinkel He 60 floatplane on the catapult and a new crane shipped for lowering and retrieval. Abaft the after funnel mantle more aerial outriggers have been fitted.

Left, upper: The Heinkel 60 being retrieved by crane.

Left, lower: A starboard view of the Heinkel 60 and catapult.

Left, upper: A stern view of *Königsberg* in 1936. On the quarterdeck a divisional parade is taking place. Ths ship is lying to a buoy, her accommodation ladder has been let down, and the propeller guard is extended. At the foretop she wears an admiral's command flag. Note the dark paintwork on the turret tops.

Left, lower: A view from the same angle two years later. The aerial outriggers abaft the after funnel have been replaced by a pole mast with crosstrees.

Above and below: *Königsberg* in 1938 after the forward fire control plus rangefinder had been installed immediately forward of the battlemast. This structure included a test site for a primitive radar room, the static antenna being fixed to the forward face of the housing. The radar image relayed the field ahead only. The two photographs show the equipment from different perspectives.

Left, upper: *Königsberg* failed to return from the invasion of Norway. Whilst lying alongside the German Bridge at Bergen she was hit by British Skua dive-bombers and sank at the quayside. This photograph shows the cruiser on fire and listing to port immediately after being hit.

Left, lower: Shortly afterwards the cruiser settled with an increased list. In the foreground is a Ju 52 floatplane with apparently unconcerned flight crewman.

Above: Another view of the burning *Königsberg*.

Right: *Königsberg* still afloat, as seen from ahead.

Above: The cruiser capsized in ten fathoms. One of her propellers juts out of the water.
Below: The end. On the quayside all that remains are a few strips of canvas.
Right, upper and lower: Salvage work began in 1941. After refloating, the wreck was towed first to Hagenaes and later to Laksvaag. The upper photograph shows the resurfaced hull, the lower a view of the leading tugs during the tow to Hagenaes.

Left, upper and lower: With the help of twenty-six 100-tonne pontoons—one of which is seen on the left in the upper photograph—the hull was stabilised and then raised. At bottom right one of the torpedo tube sets can be seen.

Above: The two propellers and rudder.
Below: The hull floating keel-up, seen from ahead. In the foreground, the aperture at the forefoot is for the extendible boom from which the paravanes were streamed.

Karlsruhe

The building contract for Cruiser 'C' (Replacement *Medusa*) was placed with Deutsche Werke, Kiel, in 1925 under Yard Number 207. The first keel material was laid on 27 July 1926. The hull was launched as *Karlsruhe* on 20 August 1927, the baptismal speech being delivered by the *Bürgermeister* of Karlsruhe and the naming ceremony performed by the widow of *Fregattenkapitän* Köhler, commander of the first *Karlsruhe*, which was lost in the Caribbean in 1914. On 15 October 1929 shipyard personnel put the cruiser through her first machinery trials, after which she transferred to Wilhelmshaven for completion. She entered service there on 6 November 1929 under *Fregattenkapitän* Eugen Lindau, her ship's company boarding from the decommissioning cruiser *Berlin*.

Prewar Service

In the months after entering service *Karlsruhe* worked up in the Baltic and on 15 January 1930 maintained a speed of 29kt for three hours. From the outset the cruiser was scheduled as a cadet training ship, and on 24 May she left Wilhelmshaven for her first overseas cruise. Her route took her through the Mediterranean to East Africa, rounding the Cape of Good Hope to South-West Africa and across to South America, the ship returning via Spain to Kiel on 12 December. The 'K' class cruisers were not built for use in tropical seas, and their use as training ships—especially *Karlsruhe*—was an expedient. In long periods at sea, particularly in the Pacific, the ship often ran short of fresh water and the extremely high humidity led to ventilation problems in the engine rooms.

The periods between foreign cruises—*Karlsruhe* sailed on four more—were used for recruit training, general exercises, trials and shipyard overhauls. Structural changes included replacing the tall pole mast by a staff at the rear of the foretop and installing single-storey deckhouses between the funnels and forward of the after deckhouse. *Kapitän zur See* Erwin Wassner became the cruiser's second commander in September 1931. On 30 November that year *Karlsruhe* left Wilhelmshaven on her second cruise. She carried aboard 524 men—30 officers, 27 warrant officers, 58 cadets and 409 other rates and civilian tradesmen.

Her route took her to the West Indies (when visiting Cuba a *Windflügelflugzeug*—'wind-wing aircraft', or helicopter—was seen for the first time and a note made) Mexico, Venezuela, the Panama Canal, Honolulu and North America, south to Cape Horn and north to New York, then Kiel. Before the cruiser put in on 8 December 1932, *Admiral* Raeder and *Konteradmiral* Schultze, Commander Training Inspectorate, came aboard to inspect the ship. This was standard practice for all German warships returning from a foreign cruise. After a brief stay at Kiel *Karlsruhe* moved to Flensburg-Mürwik, where the cadets were disembarked to undergo their final examinations at the Naval College. In December *Fregattenkapitän Freiherr* Wilhelm Harsdorf von Enderndorf was appointed the cruiser's third commander.

During 1933 the bridge-deck platforms were enlarged and two additional 8.8cm flak single mountings were installed either side of the after deckhouse. On 6 October 1933 *Konteradmiral* Saalwächter, Commander Training Inspectorate, visited the cruiser, and after Fleet Commander *Admiral* Förster made his inspection on 14 October *Karlsruhe* sailed for East Asia via Suez, then to Honolulu, the Pacific Coast of the United States, Panama, Boston and via Spain to Germany, anchoring in the Schillig Roads to collect *Admiral* Raeder on 15 June 1934 for the last leg of the voyage to Kiel. *Kapitän zur See* Günther Lütjens was appointed the fourth commander of the cruiser in September. Structural changes involved replacing the portside derrick and gear by a bar crane and discarding the stylised eagle and swastika emblems abaft the rearmost scuttles either side of the hull in favour of a single emblem on the counter.

After stabiliser keel tests at the Naval Arsenal on 5 October 1934, *Karlsruhe* cast off on the 22nd for her fourth overseas cruise via the Azores to South America, then to Cape Horn and to the Pacific coasts of America. At Callao the cruiser took part in the celebrations to mark the 400th anniversary of the founding of the Peruvian state (25 January–6 February) before making passage through the Panama Canal to visit ports on the Atlantic seaboard of the United States. *Karlsruhe* returned to Kiel on 15 June

1935. In a shipyard refit the aerial booms on the after funnel were replaced by a mast with crosstrees and the battlemast platforms were further enlarged. A catapult was installed and trials with a floatplane were held in Kiel Bay on 23 September, but the aircraft was not carried on the fifth voyage.

The cruiser's fifth captain, *Kapitän zur See* Leopold Siemens, took command in September and after the usual inspections *Karlsruhe* sailed on 21 October with 606 men aboard. At Tenerife on 7 November the cruiser became the first German naval unit to hoist the new *Reich* War Flag. She next visited São Tomé, Lobito, Durban and Port Victoria in the Seychelles.

The voyage continued to Batavia, Indonesia, Ilo-Ilo, Hong Kong and Nagasaki (where the gun crews were given an eight-day exercise), and to Kobe until 12 March. When the cruiser sailed that day, the barometer was falling. As she got further into the Pacific the wind rose gradually to Force 9 and fierce squalls swept the ocean. Huge rolling seas threatened to capsize the ship, causing her to heave-to for safety. On the 14th the storm abated for a few days, but it returned with a vengeance on the 18th when winds of hurricane Force 12 were recorded. The ship rolled and yawed alarmingly, pounding and groaning at the seams, and eventually a longitudinal frame buckled; others followed on the night of 19 March. At the level of the boat deck a fissure stretched from one side of the hull to the other, passing through the commander's cabin. When the ship plunged this rent gaped open 20mm, and whether the cruiser would survive or break apart and founder with all aboard rested in the hands of the gods. The hurricane reached the height of its fury on 20 March, by which time *Karlsruhe*, low on fuel, was heading for shelter in the Aleutians.*

The storm blew itself out on the 21st, and the cruiser reached Dutch Harbor on the 23rd. She spent five days patching up with shipboard tools and left on 7 April to repair at the San Diego US naval base, where the cracks were welded and extra I-beams bolted externally to provide additional support to the deformed hull. She left for home on 17 April, calling at Balboa, Panama and St Thomas and anchoring off Wilhelmshaven on 8 June for the usual formal inspection. Hitler came aboard on the 11th. The cadets disembarked at Flensburg between 17 and 19 June, leaving *Karlsruhe* free to enter the yards at Kiel for a scheduled refit and to complete repairs to the storm damage. The near-disaster led to the termination of her career as a cadet training ship, and she was placed at the disposal of the BdA on 1 July. Structural changes involved the erection of deckhouses between the forefunnel and battlemast and between the catapult and forefunnel. The after deckhouse was enlarged sternwards as a flak direction centre with rangefinder. A small pole mast was fitted off-centre to starboard on the forward bulkhead of the housing, while 8.8cm flak twins replaced the original single mountings. Signal wings were added to the bridge deck and a platform was installed aft of the battlemast near the searchlight podium.

On 9 September the cruiser ran the usual trials after leaving the yards and then began working up in the Baltic. Following the outbreak of civil war in Spain, *Karlsruhe* was one of the German warships appointed to patrol the Spanish coast to assist refugees and control contraband. On 27 December 1936 she left for Spanish waters and on 1 January refuelled at El Ferrol.

The cruiser penetrated the Mediterranean as far as Melilla and then patrolled the Atlantic coast between Tangiers and El Ferrol, returning to Kiel on 22 February. On 17 June 1937 she sailed again for El Ferrol, but was recalled when the German Navy withdrew its units from the international control arrangement following the Republican attacks on *Deutschland* and *Leipzig*. *Karlsruhe* arrived at Kiel on 30 June. Throughout the remainder of the year she exercised and ran trials, taking part in the Fleet manoeuvres in the central Baltic between 20 and 25 September.

On 20 May 1938 *Karlsruhe* was decommissioned for a major refit at Wilhelmshaven. This was occasioned by the experiences of the three 'K' class cruisers over the years, particularly as regards their relatively weak construction, poor stability and the lessons learned from the near-disaster in the Pacific in 1936. The major alterations were as follows. The foretop was reduced from double- to single-storey, the staff on the foretop was replaced by a mast and the searchlight platform on the battlemast was raised, a new platform being installed below it. The lower platform at the rear of the battlemast was also raised. The after funnel was shortened, and slightly canted caps were fitted to both funnels. The derrick post with searchlight stations was unshipped and searchlight platforms were erected abreast the funnels. A large bent-arm crane was

---

* The *Reich* was short of foreign currency and avoided purchasing fuel in foreign ports or from foreign companies and ships. On these overseas cruises a chartered German tanker (in this case *Mittelmeer*) accompanied the warship. This was useful for learning the techniques of refuelling at sea, as was necessary for a world power possessing no naval bases.

installed on the starboard side and a straight-arm crane on the portside. A taller mainmast with long tripod legs was fitted. The starboard hawsehole was sealed and replaced by a deck cluse. Twin 10.5cm weapons replaced the 8.8cm twin flaks and a 10.5cm single was fitted on the aft superstructure deck. Finally, anti-mine gear was fitted at the forefoot, with a shaft for the extension pole. The removal of the cruising diesel reported in one publication is improbable since the post-refit blueprints show it in place.

World War II

Karlsruhe was recommissioned by *Kapitän zur See* Friedrich Rieve, her seventh and last commander, on 13 November. Enemy activity and the severe winter of 1939/40 curtailed the usual programme of trials and working-up. Virtually the whole company was fresh to the ship, and shortly before Operation 'Weserübung' in early April 1940 the BdA reported that *Karlsruhe* was not fully combatworthy.

In a minor refit in 1940 the ship received a degaussing system and the port crane was replaced by a model similar to that on the starboard side. During the preparations for 'Weserübung' the cruiser was at Bremerhaven. Rieve had been designated commander of Warship Group 4, tasked with landing occupation troops at Kristiansand and Arendal. *Konteradmiral* Schenk, Admiral Norwegian South Coast, travelled aboard her as a passenger. At 2230 on 7 April troop transports arrived at the quayside and about 1,200 men were detrained. *Oberst* Wachsmuth's Staff and units of the 210th Infantry Regiment embarked on *Karlsruhe* and her escorts, the torpedo-boats *Seeadler* and *Luchs*. A coastal artillery company was shipped on the E-boat tender *Tsingtau* and a motor-cycle troop boarded the torpedo-boat *Greif* for Arendal. Other units of the Group were seven E-boats of the 2nd Flotilla. Four merchant ships of the 1st Naval Transport Group, *Wiegand*, *Kreta*, *August Leonhardt* and *Westsee*, had left Stettin for Kristiansand on the 6th.

At 0500 on 8 April *Karlsruhe* sailed north from Bremerhaven in company with *Luchs* and *Seeadler* at 21kt, passing west of Heligoland, while *Greif*, *Tsingtau* and the E-boats headed towards Sylt. The weather was clear with little breeze and the seas were calm. Beyond Horns Reef the visibility deteriorated, allowing *Karlsruhe* and her two escorts to increase speed to gain a reserve of time. When visibility dropped to 300m, *Luchs* and *Seeadler*, sailing abeam of *Karlsruhe*, fell in line astern of her. At six that evening, with the ships ploughing towards the rendezvous point with the remainder of the Group north of

Hanstholm, visibility was down to to 30m in patches and the three vessels maintained contact by audible fog signals, radio beacons being used to fix their position. From 2115 navigation lights were set, and by midnight ultrashort-wave contact had been established with *Greif*, *Tsingtau* and the E-boats. Speed was maintained at 21kt through the fog since *Kapitän zur See* Rieve wanted to be close to Kristiansand by 0345 so that the landings could be begin punctually at 0515 on receipt of the codeword 'Weserzeit'. The curtain of fog became so thick so that even the pilot lights had to be turned on for orientation purposes.

Around 0200 signals were received reporting heavy searchlight activity and gunfire in Oslo Fjord and that the Norwegian Admiralty had extinguished all coastal lights and radio beacons. At 0300 on 9 April visibility was zero, but forty-five minutes later *Karlsruhe* sounded the 200m line three miles south of the fjord entrance. On account of the fog and the difficult inshore waters, it was adjudged imprudent to attempt to disembark troops and the squadron sailed up and down off the harbour entrance waiting for dawn. At 0442 the mists began to lift a little and some low islands were seen. At 0517, with fog horns blaring, the group set course for the harbour entrance, their navigation being confirmed by a light buoy and land being sighted at 0557. Just after 0600 the squadron was spotted by a low-flying seaplane which ignored the Germans' recognition signal. *Kapitän zur See* Rieve noted in the cruiser's War Diary: 'The fog robbed us of the element of surprise. It was already an hour after "Weserzeit" and past dawn. The Norwegian reconnaissance aircraft would definitely have reported us. In the circumstances I abandoned the plan, which had already been postponed once from 0415, to disembark the Army and naval coastal artillery units into six E-boats in the inner skerries.' Instead the torpedo-boats *Luchs* and *Seeadler* were ordered to prepare to land their troops on Odderöy, a rock fortress with relatively high cliffs which lay directly to seaward of the port of Kristiansand. On Odderöy were believed to be four 24cm howitzers and two 21cm, six 15cm and six 6.5cm guns; a mile and a half to the east was the island of Gleodden, equipped with three 15cm and two 6.5cm guns covering the naval base of Narviken in Topdals Fjord, and which had a clear field of fire on all approaching vessels. Near the Grönningen light a pilot boat was seen leading a German steamer, *Seattle* (7,399grt); shortly afterwards Odderöy fired some red signal flares, to which the Germans responded by increasing speed and bringing their gun crews to readiness.

The Norwegians opened fire on *Karlsruhe* and a 21cm shell landed just ahead of her stem. This convinced Rieve that an attempt to force his way through could end in disaster, and 7km short of Odderöy he bore off to starboard to lengthen the range while his own gunners attempted to locate the enemy emplacements.

On the Germans' first approach, the Norwegians opened fire with all batteries, their shells straddling *Karlsruhe*. Because of her head-on approach, her after turrets were masked: all that could be brought to bear were the three barrels of 'A' turret, some 10.5cm heavy flak guns and the same calibre main armament of the two torpedo-boats. Fire was initially not returned. Although the Norwegian shooting was irregular and inaccurate for the short range, it represented a danger.

The tactical situation of the German group was not favourable. The restricted waters hampered the firing of full broadsides, and continual course changes were decided upon behind a curtain of smoke. When the first German aircraft appeared and bombed Odderöy and Gleodden, *Karlsruhe* joined in with 'A' turret. This coincided with the loss of *Seattle*. The blockade-runner had left Curaçao on 4 March and after eluding the Northern Patrol had made Tromsö before anchoring in Kristiansand Fjord prior to sailing the last leg to Germany. Not realising what was afoot, the German captain mistook the German warships for British and tried to escape. He came under the fire of the Norwegian coastal batteries, was hit by a shell from a Norwegian torpedo-boat moored at Kristiansand and was then bombed by German aircraft. The ship finished up aground and burning, later drifting out to the skerries to sink.

At 0655 *Karlsruhe* made a renewed attack, firing her after turrets through a smokescreen as she turned to port. The shipboard aircraft was catapulted off to report on the effects of the bombing of the two Norwegian strongpoints. When the German ships were within 6.5km of Oddenöy the island's batteries opened a heavy fire, straddling *Karlsruhe* and *Tsingtau*. Because of the expenditure of ammunition during the head-on approaches, shells were being passed manually from the after turrets to 'A' turret. At 0723 the German ships turned off to starboard heading north-east, which allowed *Karlsruhe* to fire her full broadside; the other German units also fired in passing. When the *Luftwaffe* made a fresh appearance, the German naval force withdrew behind a smokescreen.

At 0750 the torpedo-boats *Luchs* and *Seeadler* were ordered to land troops on Odderöy while *Karlsruhe* gave covering fire. The two boats passed Grönningen and

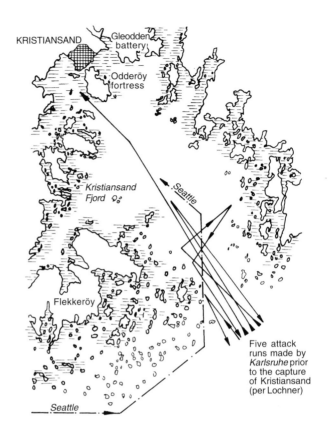

Above: The occupation of Kristiansand, 9 April 1940.

Oksöy at high speed before running into a thick fog bank and had to be recalled by Morse lamp.

The fourth approach began at 0925 through thick fog, *Karlsruhe* narrowly avoiding a reef by throwing her rudder hard to port and putting her port engine full ahead. After this scare the group turned back again.

The fog began to lift at about 1000 and the coastal artillerymen disembarked from *Tsingtau* into E-boats alongside. At about the same time *Greif* signalled that Arendal was in German hands. This broke the tension, and *Karlsruhe* received orders to proceed into Kristiansand. The German squadron passed Odderöy, eerily silent, at high speed and anchored in the inner harbour of the port. At 1220 assault troops reported the surrender of the Oddenöy batteries. *Karlsruhe* disembarked her troops into torpedo-boats and E-boats alongside.

At 1700 *Oberst* Wachsmuth reported that the city had fallen and that *Karlsruhe*'s task had therefore been completed satisfactorily. All German naval units participating in the invasion of Norway were under instructions to sail

111

for Germany as early the same day as circumstances allowed, and at 1900 on 9 April the cruiser weighed anchor for home at 21kt escorted by *Luchs*, *Seeadler* and *Greif*. Visibility was good, wind light north-easterly and the sea fairly calm. At 1930 the commander of the submarine HMS *Truant* saw to his surprise 'three destroyers [actually the three torpedo-boats] with a 'K' class cruiser in their middle'. They were running at high speed on a zig-zag course. The submarine was in an unusually favourable shooting position and fired a fan of four torpedoes at the cruiser from a range of 4,000m. The submarine then dived to 100m, where she escaped the subsequent hunt by the torpedo-boats.

Karlsruhe's War Diary records:

1900	Sunny, light wind, calm sea. Group East ordered departure while still light: (1) Sail earliest after mission completed. (2) If possible pass east of Skagen before dark. My decision: Sail at 21kt to enable T-boats to zig-zag.
1951	Course 147°, 21kt. After leaving Fjord, zig-zag course by *Karlsruhe*.
1958	Fan of four from starboard. Order: Full ahead both, hard to port. One torpedo hit compartment V/VI. Immediately 12° list to starboard. Both engines and rudder out of action. Ship lies adrift. Order 'Make smoke' not carried out as smoke unit not readied. First report by Executive Officer (IO) to Commander: 'Several sections out of action. Situation very bad. Suggestion: T-boats alongside to evacuate some of the crew. All life-saving apparatus readied for use. Motorised boats cannot be lowered as electrical plant out of action!' Second Report IO to Commander: 'Compartments III–VII flooded. Compartment VIII making water. All pumping gear out of action. Ship sinking slowly.' Decision: Evacuation of crew since ship cannot be saved. Secret papers destroyed or brought aboard T-boats. Several submarine alarms. Opened fire with machine guns and fired torpedoes. T-boats also giving submarine alarm, dropping depth charges and firing with 2cm weapons. Ship's company abandoned cruiser with great discipline and taken aboard *Seeadler* and *Luchs*.
2110	After crew had left ship, Commander and Navigation Officer transferred from *Luchs* to *Greif*, which had no *Karlsruhe* crewmen aboard, to witness sinking.
2114	*Luchs* and *Seeadler* made for Kiel on orders of BSN [Commander Coastal Defence Forces North Sea].
2230	Sea up to rail of *Karlsruhe* quarterdeck.
2245	As *Karlsruhe* could not be saved, I gave order to sink ship with a torpedo.
2250	First torpedo hit *Karlsruhe* in bow compartment XV, second torpedo at base of mast. After a few minutes *Karlsruhe* sank by the bow, starboard side.

At the fatal moment, *Karlsruhe* was heading south from Kristiansand Fjord towards the Skagen lightvessel. She and her three escort vessels were making 21kt and zig-zagging. It was known that British submarines were active in the Skagerrak and extra lookouts had been posted, but the danger was thought to be off Oslo Fjord because of the number of merchant sinkings and confirmatory reports made by reconnaissance aircraft. At 1958 *Luchs*, on the cruiser's starboard beam, gave a submarine alarm on bearing 90 degrees. *Kapitän zur See* Rieve ordered hard to port and both ahead full, but before the orders could be put into effect he saw the two torpedoes racing towards his ship. One exploded into the starboard side at compartment V/VI. The cruiser lost way quickly and assumed a list to starboard of 12°. The IO sprinted towards the stern and above compartment IV received the Chief Engineer's report that the rooms containing the main starboard turbine, the auxiliary machinery, the rudder mechanism and the port and starboard electrical plant were flooded. Access aft beyond compartment VI was not possible.

The IO reported to the commander that the ship had received a very serious hit and that she was settling slowly. On his second passage through the ship he observed that water was rising in compartment VIII, that boiler room I had been evacuated and that the magazines in compartment III were flooding. The pumps appeared to be ineffective. For these reasons, only fifteen minutes after the torpedo struck Rieve was convinced that *Karlsruhe* could not be saved. Compartments III–II were flooded: the ship's double bottom had been ripped open and repair was impossible; and the pumps were not operational because there was no current. The cruiser had settled so deeply by the stern at this point that water was pouring into the ship through the starboard scuttles and more than 2,500 tons of seawater was washing around below decks. Accordingly he decided to abandon the ship, and later gave *Greif* the order to deliver the *coup de grâce* with torpedoes.

The reports regarding the sinking of the *Karlsruhe* were sifted through in the various command centres and the following opinions and judgements were handed down:

In the War Diary of the cruiser *Karlsruhe* after the torpedo hit I find no mention of:
(a) immediate attempts to have a T-boat take the ship in

tow and get her towards the nearby Vp-boats and M-boats of the 2nd Minesweeping Flotilla for assistance;

(b) attempts to salvage valuable weapons and equipment;

(c) considerations as to how *Karlsruhe*, which was still afloat three hours after being torpedoed and needed another two torpedoes before she eventually went down, might have been towed into Kristiansand or grounded in the shallows at Jammer Bucht.

These questions have still to be examined by the BdA and Fleet Commander . . .

[Signed] Carls

[*Admiral* Carls, CO Naval Group East]

Konteradmiral Schmundt, BdA and Rieve's immediate superior, wrote on 3 May 1940:

. . . The actual condition of the ship cannot be established because she sank. The damage inflicted on her can only be assessed from the written opinions of crew members, and inaccuracies in these reports will distort our reflections on the matter today . . . It must not be forgotten that here we have a ship still in the initial stages of working-up after a lengthy period decommissioned, which was by no means battle-ready and was only being used operationally under urgent necessity. No doubt a fully trained crew would have handled the circumstances more sure-handedly and with greater conviction. If we are talking of the 'cold-blooded handling' of a situation, it is not a matter of lack of courage but of belief technically in what they were doing. The state of readiness of the ship was such that errors and omissions had to be reckoned with from the very outset . . . from statements made subsequently about the state of the machinery, if it had been properly handled and the weather remained as it was the ship probably would not have foundered . . . it was on the basis of the reports made by his IO and Chief Engineer that the commander saw the situation of his ship as hopeless . . . the commander himself is convinced that although the T-boat leader offered him a tow, he is not accountable for [not accepting] it.

[Signed] Schmundt

On 30 July 1940 the Fleet Commander, *Vizeadmiral* Lütjens, delivered a devastating condemnation of the *Karlsruhe*'s commander, IO and crew:

The measures taken after the ship was torpedoed, especially damage control, show a series of inadequacies and errors which cannot be blamed on the missing later stages of shipboard training. What was really lacking was the central direction of the damage control parties by the IO. His opinion that the ship was doomed proved incorrect, for although no measures whatever were taken to keep her afloat, she actually was still afloat two hours after being torpedoed and did not sink until two more torpedoes had been fired into her.

The decision of the commander to scuttle his ship was based on his IO's report that the cruiser was going to sink. For that reason he dismissed the offer to take the cruiser in tow since that to him would have put the towing boats in jeopardy from a fresh submarine attack. Even salvaging valuable weapons and equipment from on board took second place to avoiding losses and casualties aboard other units assisting in the endeavour.

From statements made by crew members involved, the picture emerges that a tow would probably have succeeded. I would not have thought the commander blameworthy if, at the time and place in question, he firmly believed that his ship was sinking quickly, and having refused the, for him, hopeless towing and salvage efforts for the purpose of saving other vessels and lives, he took the grave decision to scuttle his own ship. On the other hand, in agreement with Commander Group East, I would have approved an attempt to have T-boats take the cruiser in tow despite the existing danger from submarines.

The report by the IO that the ship was in a sinking condition was not correct. If the IO, instead of allowing himself to be influenced by various centres aboard ship, had taken charge of the damage control and directed the necessary operations, perhaps he might have taken a different view of things and made a different report. If I absolve him from blame it is because, as was the case with the whole ship's company, training and experience was lacking. But yet I cannot disabuse myself of the impression that the will was lacking to come to grips with the situation and so save the ship.

[Signed] Lütjens

These reports were all forwarded to the CinC, *Grossadmiral* Raeder, whose observations were recorded thus by an aide:

My opinion: The necessary effort to save the ship was not made. The impression of a hopeless situation and the fear of assumed enemy presence which might have led to further casualties offer an explanation for the commander's decision but do not justify it. The attempt to bring the ship in should have been made.

Above: The light cruiser *Karlsruhe* (i), 4,900 tons, was the most successful World War I regular-cruiser commerce raider in terms of the number of mercantile victims and tonnage sunk. She was launched at Germania Werft, Kiel, on 11 November 1912 and entered service on 15 January 1914. On 14 June 1914 she sailed from Kiel for the East American Station, relieving *Dresden* at Port-au-Prince on 25 July. On 4 August *Fregattenkapitän* Köhler was ordered to work the ship as a commerce raider. In the Central Atlantic between 18 August and 28 October 1914 *Karlsruhe* captured seventeen merchant vessels totalling 76,618grt. Of these, sixteen, of 72,225grt, were sunk and *Farn*, 4,393grt, was used as a supply tender until interned at Puerto Rico on 12 January the following year. On the evening of 4 November 1914, while steaming north from the Amazon delta to bombard Barbados, the ship was destroyed by an internal explosion, probably in the torpedo room; 263 men were lost. The 146 survivors arrived in Germany on 6 December 1914 aboard the supply ship *Rio Negro*. Armament: 12 × 10.5cm guns and two torpedo tubes. Machinery: steam turbines supplied by twelve coal-fired and two oil-fired watertube boilers, speed 28.5kt. Dimensions: 139 × 13.7 × 6.2m. Complement in wartime over 400 men. The photograph shows *Karlsruhe* on Fleet duty in early 1914. The rings on the funnels were overpainted prior to sailing.

Below: The next light cruiser named *Karlsruhe* was launched at Kaiserliche Werft, Kiel, on 31 January 1916 and entered service on 15 November that year. She served with the Fleet and took part in the Ösel operation in 1917. On 19 November 1918 the cruiser proceeded to Scapa Flow, where she was scuttled by her crew on 21 June 1919. She was similar to *Königsberg* (ii) except for her experimental HP-turbine wheel-drive. The photograph shows the ship interned at Scapa Flow in company with the battlecruisers *Von der Tann* (left) and *Hindenburg* (right).

Top: The launching of the new cruiser *Karlsruhe* at Kiel on 20 August 1927 took place before a huge number of spectators. In this photograph the hull is afloat, and after being taken in tow by harbour tugs is manoeuvred to the fitting-out quay.

Above: *Karlsruhe* on 15 October 1929, passing through the Kiel Canal to Wilhelmshaven for completion work and commissioning. The shipyard flag flies at the foretop; the mercantile flag hoisted at the ensign staff indicates that the cruiser is not yet in service.

Left: *Karlsruhe* in a Wilhelmshaven lock after commissioning. Notice the dark-painted funnels. The photograph gives a good view of the unorthodox alignment of 'B' and 'C' turrets off the centreline. In accordance with German naval tradition, 'C' turret bore the name *SMS Goeben*.

115

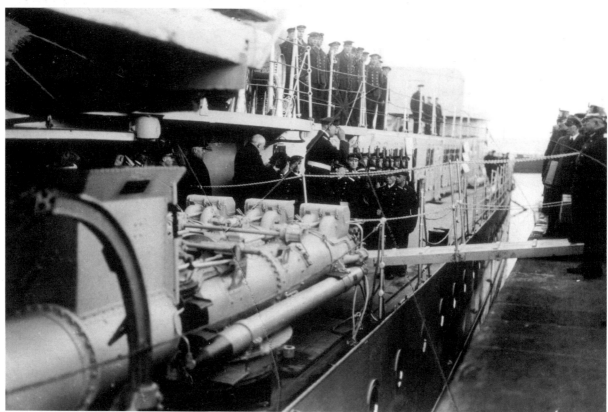

Left, upper: Shortly before leaving Kiel, a cutter is raised to davits amidships. To the left is stowed the port-side boat-mooring boom.

Left, lower: *Karlsruhe* passing through a lock chamber at Wilhelmshaven, 30 November 1931, at the commencement of her year-long overseas training cruise to the West Indies, Central America, Hawaii and the United States.

Right, upper: Accompanied by numerous motor launches, *Karlsruhe* sails from Kiel on 21 October 1935. She was absent for eight months on this, her fifth foreign cruise. Abaft the after funnel a pole mast has replaced the former aerial outriggers. The catapult installation had been unshipped to improve stability. The characteristic feature of *Karlsruhe*, distinguishing her from *Königsberg* and *Köln*, was the two-storey foretop.

Right, lower, and below: In March 1934 *Karlsruhe* visited the US naval base at San Diego. These two photographs of her arrival were taken from American aircraft.

Above: Such photographs as these were not normally released for publication in pre-war Germany. This aerial view of *Karlsruhe* amidships shows the battlemast with two-tiered foretop and rangefinder. Above the bridge is the battle command centre comprising the forward fire control and rangefinder. To the rear is the signal deck. In an open bay below the upper deck is located the starboard forward torpedo tube mounting. Between the funnels the boat deck with cradles can be seen, and on the battlemast and either side of the after funnel are searchlight platforms. The bridge platforms are screened with awnings against the strong sunlight.

Left: *Karlsruhe* seen from the air, location and date unknown. On the opposite side of the pier four accompanying torpedo-boats are made fast. The naval ensign worn by the latter indicates a date prior to 1935.

Above: *Karlsruhe* at Cristobal on 20 April 1935. Notice the new bar-crane on the port side.

Left: At Durban. On the quayside the South African public queues to visit the ship. Canvas awnings protect the decks against the strong sun. This photograph was taken before 1933 since the stern lacks the eagle and swastika emblem.

Above: Ships customarily flew a homecoming pennant when returning from long foreign cruises—and the longer the absence, the longer the pennant. Here *Karlsruhe*, signal flags fluttering and her crew paraded along the port rail in review order, is seen from the pocket-battleship *Deutschland*.
Below: Making fast at the Blücher Bridge, where numerous family members of cadets and crew await the homecoming. The first lines have been secured aboard and tugs slowly edge the cruiser to the quayside.

Above: On the forecastle preparations are in hand to cast off at the beginning of another long foreign cruise. Lining the quayside is a music corps from the *Luftwaffe*, and off-watch crewmen parade the starboard rail in review order at attention, eyes right, as a high-ranking officer leaves the cruiser.

Below: *Karlsruhe* at Kiel on 12 June 1936, flying a home-coming pennant after the fifth overseas cruise. The crew parades the starboard rail while a pinnace containing a party of high-ranking officers sets off to inspect the ship.

Left, upper: Navy Week, Kiel, June 1936: *Karlsruhe* bedecked from stem to stern with signal flags, with the *Reich War Flag* at the topmast. In the foreground is the prow and bowsprit of the training barque *Gorch Fock*.

Left, lower: *Karlsruhe* after her refit, showing one of her modern derricks. The former searchlight platforms were landed and replaced by smaller platforms on both funnels.

Above and below: Between 20 May 1938 and 13 November 1939 *Karlsruhe* was decommissioned for a major refit at the Wilhelmshaven Navy Yard. These two photographs show the cruiser after completion of the conversion. The two-tier foretop has been replaced to conform with that of her two sisters and a tripod mainmast has been installed abaft the after funnel. This funnel has been shortened, and both are now fitted with a slightly raked cowl. Modern light weapons have been mounted.

Top: *Karlsruhe* off the Norwegian coast in April 1940. In the foreground is one of the E-boats attached to her battle group.
Centre: *Karlsruhe* off Kristiansand. E-boats arrive alongside to disembark invasion troops taken on board by the cruiser in Bremerhaven.
Bottom: Late in the evening of 9 April 1940, off Kristiansand when returning to Germany, *Karlsruhe* was torpedoed by the British submarine *Truant* and so badly damaged that her captain decided she should be sunk by her escort. This photograph is one of the last of the cruiser. One of her three escorting torpedo-boats is in the foreground. The cruiser seems to be slightly down by the stern, with a small list to starboard, and the photograph may therefore have been taken after the British torpedo attack.

Köln

The contract for Cruiser 'D' (Replacement *Arcona*) was placed with Marinewerft, Wilhelmshaven, under Yard Number 116, the first keel sections being laid on 7 August 1926. *Köln* was launched on 23 May 1928 before the usual vast crowd for these occasions, the numerous guests of honour including the Mayor of Cologne, *Dr* Konrad Adenauer (in 1949 the first post-war Chancellor of West Germany), who delivered the baptismal speech. The ship was named by the widow of *Kapitän zur See* Meidinger, commander of the cruiser *Cöln* sunk in 1914. Because of the difficult economic situation the new cruiser was not completed until late in 1929. On 15 January 1930 *Kapitän zur See* Ludwig von Schröder commissioned *Köln*, her ship's company transferring aboard from the old light cruiser *Amazone*. Stoker Neumann, the only survivor from *Cöln*, was the guest of honour at the ceremony.

The first engine trials were run in the Jade from 4 February and the seaworthiness inspection was carried out by *Konteradmiral* Gladisch, BdA, in early April. In her Baltic performance trials *Köln* reached a speed of 32.5kt on 25 April. Working-up culminated in an Atlantic voyage for engine and gunnery trials from 28 October; calls were made at Las Palmas, the Cape Verde Islands and onward to Tenerife in company with *Karlsruhe* before Vigo was visited as the last stop before the return to Wilhelmshaven on 5 November. Structural changes during the year included the addition of a single-storey extension to the forward part of the after deckhouse; the erection of a single-storey deckhouse between the funnels; the replacement of the 8.8cm single flak by 8.8cm twins; and the installation of flak direction equipment abaft the after deckhouse.

Prewar Service

On 20 June 1931 *Köln* took part in the Naval Review to mark the launching of the pocket-battleship *Deutschland*. On the arrival of *Reich* President von Hindenburg the whole Fleet fired a 21-gun salute. On 14 June the cruiser left for a short summer cruise to the Norwegian fjords. *Köln* participated in the Fleet manoeuvres between 29 June and 3 July, and later in the year between 2 and 11 September. In minor refits during the year the tall pole mast was shortened and

fitted with longer signal yards, but it was later replaced altogether by a staff projecting above the rear of the foretop.

The usual programme of training and exercises began with gunnery trials off Las Palmas during a three-week Atlantic cruise beginning on 7 January 1932. The ship was inspected twice between 30 March and 4 April, by the BdA on detachment from the Fleet and by the Commander Naval Training. On 26 May, at Wilhelmshaven, Adolf Hitler, then merely leader of the NSDAP, was received aboard the cruiser. No breach of protocol was committed. Hitler often stayed at nearby Rüstringen with Senator Heinrich Picker between election campaigns. On 26 July 1932, while exercising her gun crews in the Baltic, *Köln* assisted in the attempts to salvage the sail training ship *Niobe* in the Fehmarn Belt. The barque had capsized and sunk in strong winds with many cadets aboard.

During the year one 8.8cm flak twin was landed and a signal wing was added to the bridge deck. The extensions to the after deckhouse and the deckhouse between the funnels were discarded.

In September 1932 *Fregattenkapitän* Otto Schniewind became *Köln*'s second commander. The Fleet Commander was aboard between the 16th and 21st of that month for a brief visit to Stavanger, Norway. The cruiser then spent a month in drydock. After steaming trials she prepared for her first world cruise, for which she left on 8 December. Her first stop was Caraminal, Spain, where she remained until 27 December.

The world cruise proceeded as follows. In January the ship visited Messina, Alexandria and Suez; in February Madras and Sabang; in March Java, Fremantle and Adelaide; in April Fort Phillipsbay, Melbourne and Hobart; in May Sydney and Fiji; in June Rabaul, Guam and Kobe (where from 3 to 5 July she spent time in drydock); later in July Dairen, the former German colony of Tsingtau and China; in August Shanghai, Makassar and Celebes; in September Singapore, the Straits of Malakka and Sumatra; in October Colombo and Port Said; and in November Crete (meeting up with *Karlsruhe*), Corfu and then Taranto, the Straits of Messina and Gibraltar, remaining at Vigo from 30 November to 7 December.

On 12 December *Admiral* Raeder and Commander Naval Training embarked for the entry into Wilhelmshaven, where, in Entrance III lock chamber, a huge welcome led by *Reich* Chancellor Adolf Hitler, *Reichswehr* Minister Blomberg and entourage were waiting. On 18 December *Köln* disembarked her cadets at Flensburg-Mürwik and then entered the yards for a refit.

On 1 January 1934 *Köln* was returned to Fleet duty. She ran the usual engine trials after leaving the yards on 22 March under her third commander, *Kapitän zur See* Werner Fuchs. On 7 June *Köln* and the pocket-battleship *Deutschland* sailed for gunnery exercises in the Western Atlantic. Visits were paid to Madeira, Cascais and Lisbon before the ships returned to Wilhelmshaven on 9 July. While at moorings at Kiel on 4 August the ship's company swore the oath of allegiance to Adolf Hitler following the death of *Reich* President Hindenburg. The remainder of the year was spent in routine drill in the North Sea and Baltic before the cruiser entered the Wilhelmshaven yards on 2 November for a refit which lasted until 27 December. Structural changes included the installation of a platform on the battlemast forward, at the level of the lower bridge deck, and lengthening the boom of the port-side derrick.

Throughout 1935 *Köln* exercised close to German waters in the North Sea and Baltic. On 26 and 27 July Hitler, who was very interested in naval artillery, spent two days aboard the cruiser observing gunnery exercises in Eckernförde Bay. From 27 September until 8 November *Köln* was in drydock at Wilhelmshaven, and she spent the next few months working back to full efficiency. Structural changes had included the fitting of a platform at searchlight level at the rear of the battlemast, raising the signal wings on the bridge by half a deck and extending the bridge deck to abaft the battlemast. An aircraft catapult was installed between the funnels, and the port-side derrick and gear were replaced by a shipboard crane for aircraft work. The after deckhouse was rebuilt to larger dimensions, with a pole mast of increased height and the after rangefinder re-sited further aft to make way for an elevated flak direction post. This had a light pole mast forward and off-centre to starboard, to bridge height. The twin 8.8cm guns were replaced by a newer model. The outriggers on the after funnel were discarded and rigged on a short-legged tripod mast. The ship's fourth commander, *Fregattenkapitän* Otto Backenköhler, was appointed in October.

Between 20 February and 4 March 1936 *Köln* was given the unusual task of fishery protection, anchoring in Malanger and other Norwegian fjords. On 15 April, in company with *Nürnberg* and *Leipzig*, the cruiser exercised in the Atlantic, calling at Madeira and Lagos, Portugal, before returning to Wilhelmshaven on 8 May. Between 28 and 30 May *Köln* was present at Kiel with the major part of the Fleet for the dedication by Hitler of the naval memorial at Laboe.

On 18 July civil war broke out in Spain, and German warships were given the task of evacuating German citizens from the danger area, although assistance was never refused to other nationalities requesting it. On 27 July *Köln* and the 2nd Torpedo-Boat Flotilla left Wilhelmshaven for Spain, where they patrolled the Biscay coast, returning to Wilhelmshaven on 26 August. The cruiser was drydocked between 3 and 22 September and was present at Wilhelmshaven for the launching of the battleship *Scharnhorst* on 3 October. On the 5th *Köln* made her second departure for Spanish Biscay ports, returning to Kiel on 1 December, where she was drydocked the same day until the 9th.

An International Non-Intervention Commission came into existence in 1937 in which the warships of four nations (Britain, France, Germany and Italy) agreed to maintain a general control of allotted sectors off the Spanish coast. Germany accepted responsibility for the stretch between Oropesa and Cabo de Gata, Almeria. On 5 January 1937 *Köln* sailed in company with *Deutschland* for her third patrol in Spanish waters. Severe icing was encountered in winter storms in the Bay of Biscay. After operating off Cape Ortegal, the cruiser worked into the Mediterranean as far as Melilla on the North African coast and returned to Wilhelmshaven on 15 March.

On 29 May, off Ibiza, *Deutschland* was attacked by Republican aircraft and badly damaged. Casualties were 31 dead and 110 injured, 71 of them seriously. On 7 June *Köln* sailed on her fourth patrol to Spain and made stops at El Ferrol, Lagos and Cadiz before arriving at Gibraltar on 24 June to collect *Deutschland*'s wounded. These disembarked at Wilhelmshaven on the 29th. *Köln* then drydocked at Kiel for a refit from 30 June to 19 July, sailing on 30 July for her fifth and last Spanish patrol. After a visit to Lagos *Köln* made a tour of Italian ports and exercised off Cadiz before putting back to Wilhelmshaven on 8 October. The cruiser drydocked at Kiel between the 20th and 26th of the month. In refits the aircraft catapult was replaced by a new deckhouse. The shipboard crane was landed and the smaller version switched sides with the starboard derrick. The platform at searchlight height to the rear of the battlemast was removed. *Kapitän zur See* Theodor Burchardi became *Köln*'s fifth commander in October.

From 21 February 1938 *Köln* held a four-day exercise in the North Sea with *Küstenfliegergruppe 406* before taking up fishery protection duties off the Norwegian coast, visiting Kristiansand between 7 and 9 March wearing the *Reichsdienstflagge* (Reich Service Flag) at the foretop. The duties concluded on 13 March. *Köln* was at Kiel and formed part of the Naval Review on 22 August on the occasion of the launching of the heavy cruiser *Prinz Eugen* in the presence of Hitler and the Hungarian Regent, Admiral Horthy. After a ten-day refit at Deutsche Werke, Kiel, at the beginning of September, *Köln* returned there on 31 October and remained until the New Year.

In February 1939 *Köln* was at Hamburg for the launch of the battleship *Bismarck*. On 23 March the cruiser formed part of the large Fleet operation which restored Memel to the *Reich*, and in May she accompanied all three pocket-battleships, the battleship *Gneisenau* and numerous destroyers and torpedo-boats on a major Atlantic exercise. *Köln* then visited Lisbon, returning on 17 May to the Baltic.

World War II

On 25 August 1939 *Köln* left Kiel as part of *Vizeadmiral* Densch's huge naval force to take up a waiting position between Bornholm and the Bay of Danzig in a vain attempt to prevent the break-out of Polish naval units from the Baltic. On 1 September, together with *Leipzig* and *Nürnberg*, the cruiser moved back into the North Sea, where between 3 and 18 September she helped lay the *Westwall* mine barrier between the Dutch coast and the Skagerrak

On 8 October, in company with nine destroyers, *Köln* escorted the battleship *Gneisenau* on an anti-shipping foray into the northern North Sea. Nothing was achieved and the group returned to Kiel on the 10th. On 1 and 2 November she exercised alone in the Baltic before joining forces with *Leipzig* and the 6th Torpedo-Boat Flotilla for anti-contraband patrols in the Skagerrak. On 12 December *Köln* sailed with *Leipzig* and *Nürnberg* (flagship of new BdA, *Konteradmiral* Lütjens) to escort home five destroyers returning from a minelaying sortie off the Tyne.* *Köln* was the only cruiser of the three to escape being torpedoed, and Lütjens came aboard her for the voyage home. She continued as his flagship until May 1940, when *Konteradmiral* Schmundt replaced him. There were no further activities in the year, although at Christmas Fleet Commander *Admiral* Marschall visited the ship with Deputy *Führer* Rudolf Hess.

The severe winter of 1939/40 restricted Fleet movements generally. *Kapitän zur See* Ernst Kratzenberg became the

cruiser's sixth commander in January. At the end of March *Köln* prepared at Wilhelmshaven for Operation 'Weserübung', for which she was flagship of *Konteradmiral* Schmundt, BdA, leading Warship Group 3 to Bergen.† *Köln* reached the inner anchorage at Bergen unscathed before dawn on 9 April and at 0706 all her turrets returned the fire of the Sandviken battery. By 0835 these emplacements were in German hands. Once the disembarkation of troops had been accomplished successfully, *Köln* weighed anchor and formed up with the torpedo-boats *Leopard* and *Wolf*. Personnel losses were suffered during an attack by Wellington bombers before the small group sailed at 2000 on 9 April, the cruiser streaming her bow protection gear to pass through waters mined by the Norwegian minelayer *Tyr*. Because of enemy air activity, the group anchored in Mauranger Fjord overnight and sailed eventually at 1845 the next day. Before dawn on 11 April the destroyers *Hermann Schoemann* and *Richard Beitzen* came up from the German Bight, and all five units reached Wilhelmshaven safely.

There were no further missions during the year and *Köln* remained in the Baltic. From 26 June to 10 August she was laid up at Deutsche Werke, Kiel, and once Operation 'Seelöwe'—the proposed invasion of Great Britain—had been cancelled in September she continued her refit at Gotenhafen from 19 November until well into 1941. Structural changes included the removal of the after torpedo-tube mountings and the installation of a degaussing system. A 15m² wooden helicopter pad was mounted on the roof of 'B' turret. *Köln* emerged from the yards on 28 March 1941. *Kapitän zur See* Friedrich Hüffmeier, a former commander of *Scharnhorst*, was appointed the cruiser's seventh commander in May 1941.

The aeronautical engineer Anton Flettner had first published his ideas for a helicopter in 1924 but had failed to interest the *Luftwaffe* in the concept since it appeared to them too slow for useful operational work. The German Navy recognised its value as a naval scout and observer aircraft from the beginning, funding Flettner's work from 1938 onwards. In that year he had six models under construction, the first Fl 265 having its maiden flight in May 1939. The machine had a single engine driving two intermeshing, contra-rotating motors through a gearbox, on either side of which twin-bladed rotors were located on

---

* The details of this fiasco are recounted in the career notes for *Nürnberg* and *Leipzig*.
† For further details of this operation see the career notes for *Königsberg*.

shafts. This led to a larger and more refined version, the Fl 282 *Kolibri*, with seats for two pilots. Its 150hp Siemens und Halske SH14A drive provided a top speed of 150kph. Germany was the pioneer in helicopter development, and in 1942 the *Kolibri* became the first helicopter anywhere to enter operational military service. It was very agile, and in a 20-minute trial proved it could elude two attacking fighters. The Fl 282 was the most advanced helicopter development during World War II. In early 1941 testing of the thirty prototypes commenced aboard warships, including *Köln* in the Baltic, the minelayer *Drache* in the Mediterranean and, from 17 April, the ex-Yugoslav repair ship *Zmaj*. The trials exceeded all expectations and were continued in the Baltic into 1942 aboard *Köln* and in 1943 from the submarine-chaser *UJ 1210*, the training boat for the Anti-Submarine School. When funds finally became available for mass-production in 1944 the *Kriegsmarine* and *Luftwaffe* ordered 1,000, but only about thirty could be completed.*

In early autumn 1941 *Köln* was attached to the Northern Group of the Baltic Fleet, which comprised the battleship *Tirpitz*, the cruisers *Admiral Scheer* and *Nürnberg*, three destroyers and five torpedo-boats. On 23 September *Köln* sailed from Swinemünde for the Aaland Sea to blockade the Red Fleet, returning on the 29th. Between 12 and 21 October her guns bombarded Russian positions in support of German landings on the island of Dagö. North of the island on 13 October the cruiser avoided torpedoes fired by the Russian submarine *SC-323*. On 14 October she bombarded the Estonian island of Ristna. The severe winter of 1941/42, in which the Baltic ports froze over, put an end to further activities for the year, and *Köln* transferred to the North Sea.

Korvettenkapitän Hellmuth Strobel became *Köln*'s eighth (acting) commander in March 1942. Between 5 February and 23 May the cruiser fitted out in the Wilhelmshaven yards. Structural changes included the removal of the lower searchlight platform on the derrick post and the fitting of a rangefinder radar aerial to replace the 6m rangefinder on the forward fire control stand. Following discharge from the shipyard *Köln* worked up under her ninth commander, *Kapitän zur See* Martin Baltzer, for her forthcoming employment in Norway. She sailed on 13 July and after an intermediate stop at Oslo arrived on 6 August at Narvik to relieve the heavy cruiser *Lützow*. On 10 September *Köln* moved up to Alta Fjord. Because of her poor seakeeping in heavy conditions she was not very useful for operations and was there mainly to make up the numbers, rarely straying far from her various anchorages.

Kapitän zur See Hans Meyer bacame her tenth commander in December 1942, but following Hitler's decommissioning order of 6 January *Köln* returned to Kiel, where her ensign was hauled down on 17 February.

The long retreat on the Eastern Front needed *Kriegsmarine* support seawards, and numerous decommissioned units were returned to service. In January 1944 a fresh ship's company was mustered for *Köln* and the cruiser was towed from Kiel to Königsberg dockyard to be made seaworthy. She was recommissioned on 1 April by her eleventh commander, *Fregattenkapitän* Hellmuth Strobel, but did not emerge from the yards until 1 July, when she was attached to the Training Division as a cadet training ship.

On 11th October 1944 she loaded 90 mines at Swinemünde and sailed to Oslo Fjord in company with the destroyers *Richard Beitzen* and *Friedrich Ihn*. *Korvettenkapitän (Ing)* Heye, *Köln*'s last Chief Engineer, recollects the cruiser's final months:†

> On Saturday 30 September 1944 I relinquished my post to my successor at Hohenschwangau, and after a fifteen-day journey—my marching orders were embellished with twelve visas—I found *Köln* on 14 October at Horten, the naval base at the entrance to Oslo Fjord. She had been reactivated after a long period out of commission and belonged to the Fleet Training Group. She was a clapped-out light cruiser built before 1930. All her wiring was to have been replaced in 1939; only her sister-ship *Karlsruhe* had had it done by the time war came. Consequently there was about 200km of brittle cabling, and electrical malfunctions were daily occurrences. My predecessor had brought this to the attention of the commander. The latter had never submitted an official defect report during the war and took the Chief Engineer's complaints personally. The Chief had been drafted and I was his replacement!
>
> Two days after my arrival he packed his bags and that same evening I had to prepare for the minelaying operation. *Köln*, *Emden* and the destroyers *Karl Galster*, *Richard Beitzen* and *Friedrich Ihn* were to lay the 'Augustus' minefield. Four air raids by between 25 and 40 bombers over the period 15–20 October put paid to the operation.

---

* By command of the *Führer*, an Fa 226 transport helicopter flew a secret operation from Berlin to Danzig between 26 February and 5 March 1945, returning to Werder near Berlin on 11 March 1945 after a flight of 1,675km.

† Heye was Chief Engineer of the destroyer *Erich Koellner*, sunk at Narvik on 13 April 1940. Subsequently he was CO for three years at the 2nd Naval NCO Training School, Hohenschwangau—the first and only *Kriegsmarine* technical college. The author was trained there.

I looked at the ship's company. I knew none of my watch engineers or ERAs. The ship was over-crewed. There were 900 men aboard compared with a peacetime complement of 520. Even after the change of cadets there were still about 800, of which 260 were seamen branch and 90 engineer cadets. The officer corps was overstrength and I had twelve subordinate engineer officers instead of the usual six—mostly young men who had been trained for U-boats but were no longer required. There were even junior lieutenants who had been retrained in six months from coastal artillery to the seaman branch. My watch officers had all come up through the ranks. The Executive Officer had entered the Imperial Navy in 1916 but had little shipboard experience. This meant that the commander and I were the only officers aboard who had gone through the normal, unforced peacetime naval training course. How different things were from the heady years of 1941—engine plant liable to breakdown at any moment, an officer corps simply thrown together, disgruntled warrant officers who had not been able to obtain a commission.

In the weeks after the abandoned mining operation the ship just lay in the fjord with the mines still on her side decks, changing anchorage each evening once the British reconnaissance aircraft of the day had gone home. We ran a few troopship escorts in the fjord. We were stringent about conserving fuel. In November 1944, after a grounding at Frebergvik near Horten, we went into the floating dock at Oslo. The Executive Officer was summoned ashore on some pretext and taken to Akershus fortress. Apparently he had been involved in the 20 July [Bomb] Plot in some way. Fortunately for him he did not come to trial before the war ended. We landed our 90 mines.

At Frederiksstad on the night of 13 December, towards 1900, Beaufighters from No 5 Group, Bomber Command, attacked. Our flak opened up, and, after the usual *Tannenbaum*, the bombs came down—no direct hits but a lot of near misses about 10m from the hull, causing engine damage which the Oslo yard could not repair. During the attack we had only one boiler with steam up and the cruise diesels were coupled to the propeller shafts so that we could make a quick getaway in an emergency. The anchor was heaved in straight away, the machine telegraph put to 'Slow ahead'. Nothing happened. There was insufficient air pressure to start up the diesels. Meanwhile the bombs were whistling down. The electrical plant had finally had it and more or less just collapsed. Even the emergency lighting was only a feeble glimmer. Using pocket flashlights, the stokers lit the boilers with all jets and forced the steam up (something that was permitted only in an emergency and ignoring all safety regulations), and within a few minutes we had full steam pressure to sail. As there was no current, the turbines couldn't be coupled to the drive shafts (which were still hooked up to the diesel).

The air raid lasted about twenty minutes. Finally we gor current from the generators and moved off. We used a cruising compass because it took a while to get the gyro-compass working after an electrical failure. There was a magnetic compass but for some reason this wasn't working.

The British attacked again a few minutes into the New Year. Again they registered no direct hits, but many near misses caused serious blast damage, forcing us to drydock again in Oslo. An army of sentries armed to the teeth surrounded the ship to protect her against sabotage. As it was very foggy, they fired off a volley into the air every so often. The repairs at Oslo were unsatisfactory, and on 4 January we headed for Wilhelmshaven.

On 27 January *Kapitän zur See* Strobel was ordered to the East and the new Executive Officer, *Korvettenkapitän* Fritz-Henning Brandes, became the caretaker commander. The author returned to Wilhelmshaven shortly before *Köln*'s end. The days were filled with continual air raid warnings, when the crew would repair to a large bunker in the vicinity. This was itself hit on 30 March, with dead and injured amongst civilians and dockyard workers. An air raid warning had been given and the first bombs fell very quickly afterwards. Before the 'All Clear' had been given, the crew was ordered to the ship to fight fires and salvage personal effects from the stern of the cruiser. Although the fires were not too serious, it was not possible to enter the after section because the cruiser had a huge list and was in danger of capsizing. Therefore everybody got ashore as quickly as possible. The author lost everything except the uniform he was wearing at the time. The crew were found quarters in the Roon Barracks and given clearing-up work over Easter. After being kitted out afresh on 5 April, they left Wilhelmshaven next day for Cuxhaven, finishing up at Mürwik. From there they fought on land at Neustrelitz.

The cruiser sank on an even keel in the yard basin and was decommissioned on 5 April. A party of technicians and weapons personnel remained behind at Wilhelmshaven. As the cruiser was upright, with 'B' and' C' turrets above water, flying cables were run out and 'B' turret was made ready by means of a makeshift wooden platform. These 15cm guns bombarded enemy tank formations and positions in the Varel area for a few days.

After the capitulation the wreck was broken up piecemeal when the shipyard was being dismantled. The remains were raised for scrap in 1956 during the rebuilding of the naval arsenal.

Above: The light cruiser *Cöln* (i), 4,362 tons, was launched at Germania Werft, Kiel, on 5 June 1908 and entered service on 16 June 1911. Her early career was uneventful. At the outbreak of war she was flagship of *Konteradmiral* Leberecht Maass, Commander Torpedo-Boats in the Jade. On 28 August 1914 she sailed towards Heligoland to assist a patrol surprised by a superior British naval force. In thick fog she came up against the British battlecruiser *Lion* and, finding that escape was not possible, accepted battle with her 10.5cm guns. She was overwhelmed and sunk along with the light cruisers *Mainz* and *Ariadne*. A total of 411 men were lost aboard *Cöln*. The only survivor, a stoker, was picked up after 72 hours in the water. Armament: 12 × 10.5cm and 4 × 5.2cm guns and two torpedo tubes. Machinery: steam turbines fired by fifteen coal-fired boilers, speed 26.8kt. Dimensions: 130 × 14 × 5.73m. The photograph shows the cruiser in a transit of the Kiel Canal before the war.

Below: The light cruiser *Cöln* (ii), 5,620 tons, was launched at Blohm & Voss, Hamburg, on 5 October 1916, but because of shortages of raw materials completion was delayed and she did not enter service until 17 January 1918. On 19 November the cruiser sailed to Scapa Flow, where she was scuttled by her crew on 21 June 1919. She was similar in construction to *Karlsruhe* (i) but had eight coal-fired and six oil-fired watertube boilers, giving a speed of 29.3kt. Armament: 8 × 15cm guns and 3 ×8.8cm flak, four torpedo tubes. Dimensions: 149.8 × 14.2 × 6.43m. Complement: 17 officers and 542 men. This aerial photograph shows the cruiser en route to Scapa Flow.

Above left: Launch day for the new cruiser *Köln*, 23 May 1928: representatives of the Wilhelmshaven Navy Yard welcome the guests of honour. From the left are *Vizeadmiral* Bauer (obscured); *Admiral* Zenker, Commander North Sea Station; *Konteradmiral* Franz, C-in-C Naval Command (obscured); and Groener, Senior Shipyard Director and *Reichswehr* Minister, who is in conversation with the shipyard works council—(left to right) Watermann, Rust, Peekes and Krökel. Krökel died in Neuengamme concentration camp during the war.

Above right: The guests of honour: left to right, Zenker, Groener and the Mayor of Cologne *Dr* Konrad Adenauer, later the first postwar Chancellor of the German Federal Republic.
Below: Immediately before the naming ceremony, the hull, dressed with flags from stem to stern, is ready to slide down the ways. In the background can be seen the sister-ship *Königsberg* fitting out; to the left of her, in Drydock V, is the old battleship *Schleswig-Holstein*.

Left, upper: *Köln* trundling down to the water. On Slip 1 (right) are the frames of another new cruiser, *Leipzig*.

Left, lower: *Köln* fitting out. In the foreground three new torpedo-boats are under construction—*Wolf*, *Leopard* and *Jaguar*.

Above: A view across the shipbuilding basin to *Köln* fitting out in the shadow of shipyard cranes. Her main turrets have not yet been shipped. On Slipway 1 the hull of *Leipzig* is well advanced. Notice the underwater bulge, which was not a feature of the *Königsberg* class.

Right: *Köln* with 'A' turret now installed, the roof covered by a tarpaulin. The bridge and battlemast have been rigged with signal yards and aerial booms.

133

Left: The simultaneous commissioning of *Köln* and decommissioning of the old Imperial cruiser *Amazone*, the ships lying stern-to-stern. The ceremony is completed by lowering the ensign of the latter and raising that of the former. The crew transfers from one ship to the other.

Above: After the joint ceremony, *Köln* flies the ensign and jack while *Amazone* lies deserted at the quayside.

Below left: After the ship entered service the usual intensive training and working up began under the supervision of the various technical commissions. The photograph depicts the cruiser in turning trials at 32kt. The results of these trials were tabulated so that commanders and watch officers knew the likely behaviour of the ship in most given circumstances.

Above: The flag of the cruiser *Cöln*, sunk in the Battle of the Heligoland Bight, occupied a worthy position within the new ship.

Top: A general view of *Köln* during turning trials.
Above left: The wake at full speed—always an impressive picture.
Above right: In October 1930 representatives from the city of Cologne visited the cruiser and the *Bürgermeister* of Cologne, *Dr* Konrad Adenauer, took the opportunity to address the ship's company on the quarterdeck.
Left: The war flag of the Imperial German Navy flies from the foretop pole mast on 31 May 1931—Skagerrak Day—commemorating the Battle of Jutland.

Left, top: A forward view from starboard, showing the cruiser's sheer. In the large bay amidships a torpedo tube mounting can be seen.

Left, centre: The traditional 'rowing off' of a high-ranking officer on transfer out—here Executive Officer *Korvettenkapitän* Schenk, at Wilhelmshaven Navy Yard, 29 September 1930. Schenk had been Navigation Officer, then Executive Officer, of the cruiser *Amazone* from 26 September 1927 until 15 January 1930, and Executive Officer of *Köln* since commissioning.

Left, bottom: 'A' turret gun crew. The three main turrets aboard *Köln* were named *Helgoland* ('A'), *Dogger Bank* ('B') and *SMS Goeben* ('C').

Right, upper: *Köln* stopped but not anchored. In the foreground a cutter returns to the cruiser after 'man overboard' drill; she has corresponding signal flags aloft. At the foretop pole she flies an admiral's command flag—presumably the BdA (CinC Naval Scouting Units) is aboard.

Right, lower: *Köln* during a 1931 naval review.

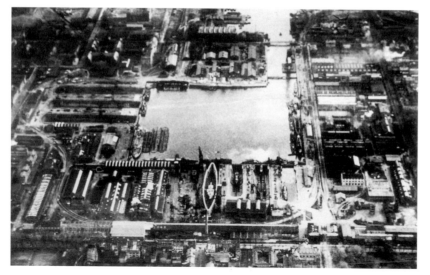

Left, top: This aerial photograph of Wilhelmshaven Navy Yard taken on 6 November 1931 shows *Köln* against the eastern quay (top) of the ship-building basin during a minor refit. On Slipway 1 opposite is the hull frame of the new pocket-battleship *Admiral Scheer*.

Left, centre and bottom: On 26 May 1932 the cruiser received an unexpected visitor when the NSDAP Party leader Adolf Hitler came aboard during an election campaign: in the centre photograph Hitler is seen in company with *Kapitän zur See* Schröder, *Köln*'s commander; in the bottom photograph he is with his retinue (including, third from the right, his publicity man Putzi Hanfstängel).

Right, upper: It is traditional that the *Grosse Wache* guard detachment is supplied by naval personnel—preferably a ship's company—on Skagerrak Day, 31 May. In 1934 the detachment was provided by the cruiser *Köln*, and it is seen here marching through a Berlin thoroughfare.

Right, lower: Navy Week, Kiel, 1935. On either side of the jetty are *Köln* and the pocket-battleship *Admiral Scheer*.

Above: Navy Week, Kiel, June 1935. For the instruction of the numerous visitors a practice torpedo is fired. In the background, right, is the gunnery training ship *Bremse*.
Below: *Köln* at the Alaska anchorage (today Nordhafen),

Wilhelmshaven, in the summer of 1935. Immediately ahead of her bow is the old battleship *Schlesien* and in the distance is the pocket-battleship *Deutschland*.

Above: *Köln* preparing to leave Entrance III, with an honour guard drawn up on the quay.
Below: The cruiser from a different angle. On the quayside a large crowd of onlookers, including family members, has assembled to wave farewell.

Above: *Köln* at Messina on 8 January 1933, dressed overall on the occasion of the birthday of the Italian Queen. The 8.8cm flak firing the salute was the model later deemed unsatisfactory and unshipped. Firing a gun in salute is an old tradition originating from the practice of warships firing off their cannon when entering a foreign harbour as a means of showing their peaceful intentions. The ceremonial of honouring foreign dignitaries developed from this in due course.

Heads of state and princes always received a 21-round salute, as did the national colours; grand admirals or officers of equal rank could expect a 19-round salute, and so on downwards. A vice-consul was entitled to only five rounds. The extent to which a warship would be be dressed overall, or the size of her colours and from where flown, was determined by similar protocol.

Below: *Köln* in India with boatloads of callers alongside.

Above: *Köln* leaving Sydney, May 1933.
Below: Short periods in dock were programmed into overseas cruises, primarily for defouling. The photograph shows *Köln* in drydock at Kobe, Japan, in July 1933.

Left: *Köln* arriving at Entrance III, Wilhelmshaven, her homecoming pennant set at the foretop.

Below: Making fast in Entrance III, Wilhelmshaven, 12 December 1933, before an honour guard and huge crowds of well-wishers. The ship's company has assembled on the upper deck . . .

Above left: . . . for a very important visit: *Reich* Chancellor Adolf Hitler inspects the cruiser. On either side of Hitler are *Admiral* Raeder, CinC Navy, and *Reichswehr* Minister *General* Blomberg, followed by other admirals and Party chiefs.

Above right: Hitler addresses *Köln*'s crew on the quarterdeck.

Left: Hitler spent more time with the Navy than is commonly believed. In August 1935 he was aboard *Köln* to observe gunnery drill. To his right is *Konteradmiral* Boehm, BdA.

Below left: *Köln* in drydock. Although cradled, all ships in drydock were given additional lateral support. Here a good view of the port-side stabilising keel is provided.

Below right: The port propeller measured against a crewman.

Left, upper: Exercise while under way at sea: *Köln* making smoke at high speed.

Left, upper and lower: Firing practice as seen forward from the battlemast. 'A' turret has just fired towards a target fine on the starboard bow; the rangefinder is of course also trained in that direction. Notice the dark-painted turret roof and its two projecting periscope optics. The white circle is the usual pre-war aircraft recognition symbol. As the rail stanchions have not been lowered this was probably an *Abkomm-schiessen*, i.e the firing of live ammunition of a smaller calibre through a special barrel jacket.

Below: After turrets 'B' and 'C' firing. Both these photographs were probably taken during a cruise in warmer climes. *Köln* was attached to the international control system set up during the Spanish Civil War, and during this period gunnery exercises were held in the Atlantic.

Right, upper and lower: 'B' and 'C' turrets firing, photographed from a different angle.

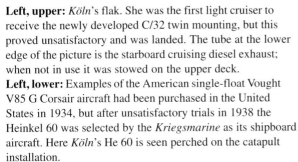

Left, upper: *Köln*'s flak. She was the first light cruiser to receive the newly developed C/32 twin mounting, but this proved unsatisfactory and was landed. The tube at the lower edge of the picture is the starboard cruising diesel exhaust; when not in use it was stowed on the upper deck.

Left, lower: Examples of the American single-float Vought V85 G Corsair aircraft had been purchased in the United States in 1934, but after unsatisfactory trials in 1938 the Heinkel 60 was selected by the *Kriegsmarine* as its shipboard aircraft. Here *Köln*'s He 60 is seen perched on the catapult installation.

Top left: The *Reich* War Flag was flown at the foretop pole mast on 1 January (New Year), 18 January (Reich Foundation Day), 30 January (day of Hitler's seizure of power), 1 March (Return of the Saar to the *Reich*), 20 April (Adolf Hitler's birthday), 1 May (Workers' Day), 31 May (Skagerrak Day; the old Imperial Ensign was flown instead of the *Reich* War Flag), 29 August (Foundation of the Prussian-German Navy, 1859), and the Sunday after Michaelmas (Harvest Thanksgiving Day). Other anniversaries were also observed—the incorporation of Austria into the *Reich*, Remembrance Day in March, and others as directed by OKM, Naval Station Command or other offices. This custom was observed by land stations and all naval units irrespective of whether they were at sea or in a German or foreign port.

Above left: Torpedo practice in Eckernförder Bay.
Above right: Physical training on the quarterdeck.
Below: The *Führer*'s Party Deputy, Rudolf Hess, visiting an NCO's mess room aboard the cruiser, Christmas 1939. Seated (left) is Fleet Commander *Admiral* Marschall.

Left, top: *Köln* icebound in Kieler Förde during the winter of 1939/40.

Left, centre: The ice was so thick in the winter of 1939/40 that communication with the shore could be maintained by means of a beaten track. Running from *Köln* amidships is 'Ernst Baecker Way', named after the Executive Officer.

Left, bottom: All three *Königsberg* class cruisers took part in the Norwegian campaign in April 1940, but only *Köln* survived. Here the cruiser is seen entering Grand Harbour, Wilhelmshaven, on 11 April 1940. Barrage balloons aloft offer a defence against low-flying aircraft.

Right, upper: *Köln* mooring with tug assistance, 11 April 1940.

Right, lower: *Köln* in the Baltic in 1940 during a BdA exercise. This photograph was probably taken from *Nürnberg*; notice, on the decking, the now standard swastika air recognition symbol.

Left, top: After the attack on Russia, *Köln* was attached to the so-called Baltic Fleet in the autumn of 1941 and bombarded Soviet installations during landings on the Baltic islands. Here 'B' turret has just fired.

Left, centre: Units of the Baltic Fleet, autumn 1941: the battleship *Tirpitz* (left) and the light cruiser *Köln*, with, in the background, a destroyer.

Left, bottom: Icebound in Kieler Förde during the winter of 1941/42, *Köln* wears the typical camouflage of the time.

Above: In 1942 *Köln* was transferred to Norwegian waters for a few months. She is seen here with her flak guns manned.

Right: An Allied aerial photograph of the cruiser at a Vaetten Fjord anchorage. The net defences are clearly evident. *Köln* is close in to the shore and apparently under camouflage netting. In combination with certain materials this afforded radar protection and confused reconnaissance fliers.

153

Above: *Köln* in Norway: a port-side view of the cruiser wearing the usual camouflage livery for these waters.

Left, upper: The end came for the cruiser on 30 March 1945 at the Wilhelmshaven Navy Yard, when she was a victim in one of the heaviest air raids on the city. Moored at the eastern corner of the shipbuilding basin, she settled on the bottom as the result of several near misses. This photograph was taken on 19 April 1945.

Left, lower: The wreck as seen by British and Polish troops on their arrival in Wilhelmshaven on 7 May 1945.

Right: Two photographs of the cruiser from different perspectives. Supplied with makeshift wooden platforms and electrical cabling, 'B' and 'C' turrets continued to engage enemy tank formations.

Left, upper: German prisoners unloading munitions.
Left, lower, and this page: Work to dismantle the wreck began shortly after the end of the war. The view left, from a crane, looks towards the site over a Soviet freighter, one of several which shipped out the Soviet entitlement to the dockyard inventory and much else besides. The remainder of the wreck was removed after Wilhelmshaven's new naval arsenal was completed in 1956.

Leipzig

The keel of Cruiser 'E' (Replacement *Amazone*) was laid on 18 April 1928 under Yard Number 117 at the Marinewerft, Wilhelmshaven, and the hull was launched as *Leipzig* on 18 October 1929. Amongst the guests at the latter ceremony were eight survivors of *Leipzig* (i), which had been lost at the Battle of the Falklands in 1914. The baptismal speech was delivered by the *Bürgermeister* of Leipzig, *Dr* Rothe. The widow of *Fregattenkapitän* Haun named the cruiser with the words 'We need a sign to save the Fatherland. On the orders of the *Reich* President I name thee *Leipzig*!'

On 8 October 1931 the ship was commissioned at Wilhelmshaven by her first commander, *Kapitän zur See* Hans-Herbert Stobwasser. Working-up, sea trials and crew training commenced at once.

Prewar Service

During 1932 the cruiser worked up in the Baltic, with numerous visits to the yards at Wilhelmshaven and Kiel for adjustment work and completion. The Acceptance Committee came aboard on 16 June. Between 6 and 16 September *Leipzig* took part in the autumn Fleet exercises.

Trials and exercises continued throughout 1933. There were foreign visits to Funchal, Madeira, from 27 February to 2 March (during the Atlantic training cruise, 21 February–15 March), to Hangö, Finland, between 23 and 28 June (during the summer training cruise, 19 June–10 July) and to Aarhus, Denmark, from 5 to 9 July, where on the 7th the Danish king, Christian X, and entourage visited the ship. A 21-gun salute was fired.

A 19-gun salute was fired on the occasion of the visit by *Reich* Chancellor Adolf Hitler, Vice-Chancellor von Papen, Goering, Goebbels and other political leaders at Kiel on 22 May to observe a night gunnery exercise. *Leipzig* took part in the autumn Fleet exercises between 11 and 22 September. On 25 September *Korvettenkapitän* Otto Hormel became her second commander.

The usual routine of exercises, yard visits and training was continued into 1934. Visits were paid from 11 to 15 July to Portsmouth and from 26 to 29 July to Reykjavik. Between 14 and 17 December *Leipzig* moored on Buoy A5 at Kiel for the removal by floating crane of the deckhouse between the funnel and battlemast to make way for the aircraft catapult installation. The horizontal aerial gaffs on the face of the funnel were removed and two larger semi-upright pylons erected on rear of the funnel.

Fleet exercises with the pocket-battleship *Deutschland*, the old battleship *Schlesien*, the light cruiser *Köln* and the 3rd Torpedo-Boat Flotilla were held in the German Bight between 25 May and 3 June 1935, when the BdA raised his flag aboard *Leipzig*. During August she was the flagship of *Konteradmiral* Boehm as various gunnery, torpedo, minelaying and searchlight exercises were held with other Fleet units. Hitler came aboard for a few days in mid-August to observe the manoeuvres. On 9 September *Fregattenkapitän* Otto Schenk became the cruiser's third commander. Later in the year the aerial gaffs at the rear of the funnel were landed and replaced by a pole mast with crosstrees.

On 14 April 1936, in company with *Nürnberg* (flag, BdA) and *Köln*, *Leipzig* exercised in the Atlantic, briefly also with the KdF liners *Der Deutsche*, *Sierra Cordoba* and *Oceana*. Las Palmas was visited between 23 and 26 April, and Lagos in Portugal between 29 April and 3 May. Catapult exercises were begun on 2 May. On the 8th of the month the shipboard Heinkel 60 capsized and was lost. *Leipzig* returned to Wilhelmshaven on 8 May and took part in the Naval Review on 28 and 29 May at Kiel attended by Adolf Hitler.

She was at Wilhelmshaven on 19 August 1936 when orders came for raising steam. Civil war had broken out in Spain the previous month and *Leipzig* was required for coastal protection duty. On 3 August the French government had proposed the setting up of an international Non-Intervention Commission in which the warships of four nations (Britain, France, Germany and Italy) would maintain a general control of all sectors of the Spanish coast, and on 24 August the four powers signed an agreement to come into effect in 1937. The *Kriegsmarine* would accept responsibility for the Mediterranean coast between Oropesa and Cabo de Gata (Almeria). The purpose of the German naval presence was the protection of German lives and property, and communication was maintained with Republican and Nationalist harbours without discrimination. Refugees were accepted for evacuation without enquiry.

On 20 August 1936 *Leipzig*, *Nürnberg* (flag, BdA), *Admiral Graf Spee* and four torpedo-boats sailed for Biscay via the English Channel and on 23 August put into Portugalete. On 1 September *Leipzig* called at San Sebastian to collect refugees for transport to St-Jean-de-Luz in France. Her offshore patrols alternated with stops, in addition those ports already mentioned, at Gijon and Corunna. On 9 September the torpedo-boats *Wolf* and *Jaguar* came alongside to take off refugees.

During September coastal patrols continued as far west as the Atlantic, with repeated visits to Corunna, to Caraminal and to the Commander of the Spanish Fleet at El Ferrol. On 26 September, off Santander, *Leipzig* sighted units of the Red Spanish Fleet—the old battleship *Jaime I*, the cruisers *Libertad* and *Miguel de Cervantes* and four destroyers. The following day six blacked-out warships were closely watched off Cape Machiaco. On 8 October *Köln* arrived to relieve *Leipzig*, and the latter arrived at Wilhelmshaven on the 10th for a scheduled refit lasting until 3 February 1937.

Trials were run in the Baltic following discharge from the yards, and on 10 March *Leipzig* sailed to relieve *Köln* at El Ferrol. After a few days of shipboard repairs at El Ferrol and in the Bay of Barquero, the cruiser rounded the peninsula, visiting Algeciras and Ceuta between 25 and 30 March. Her patrol included Mallorca, Cadiz and Tangiers before anchoring at Malaga on 12 April and the Spanish enclave of Melilla on the North African coast the next day. She remained on station in the Mediterranean until 15 May, other ports visited being Ibiza, Algiers, Cartagena, Formentera and Valencia. Her commander's War Diary for the period shows a variety of activity ranging from boarding derelicts, contraband control, monitoring movements of Republican warships and observation of shore installations and shipping. The cruiser returned to Kiel on 19 May via Biscay and the Channel.

Leipzig sailed from Kiel for Spain on 1 June 1937 and made a round voyage taking in Ibiza, Cadiz and Tangiers between 9 and 14 June. On 15 and 18 June the cruiser was the target for two mysterious torpedo attacks, apparently by a submarine, the responsibility for which was never admitted. As a consequence of this and the serious attack on *Deutschland* at Ibiza on 29 May by Red aircraft, Germany withdrew from the international Non-Intervention Committee and took no further part in the official coastal patrols, although she maintained a naval presence in Spanish waters until the civil war ended in 1939.

The cruiser left the Mediterranean on 19 June 1937 and made stops at Cadiz and Lagos on the return to Biscay, docking at the Deutsche Werke, Kiel, from 29 June until 4 August. The usual pattern of training drills and exercises ensued. On 17 September the BdA, *Konteradmiral* Densch, hoisted his flag aboard *Leipzig* for the big *Wehrmacht* manoeuvres between 20 and 25 September. On 11 October the cruiser entered the Baltic for various exercises and routine protocol visits and remained there for the rest of the year. *Kapitän zur See* Werner Löwisch became the cruiser's fourth commander in October.

A full programme of training, exercises and shipyard lay-ups occupied the first eight months of 1938. On 22 August *Leipzig* formed part of the Naval Review before Hitler and the Hungarian Vice-Regent Admiral Horthy on the occasion of the launching of the heavy cruiser *Prinz Eugen* at Kiel; she was also at Kiel on 8 and 9 December for the launch of the aircraft carrier *Graf Zeppelin*. During the year the angular crane on the port side was replaced by one of straight design. The cruiser entered Deutsche Werke, Kiel, for a refit on 17 December and remained there until 15 March 1939.

For the restoration of Memel to the German *Reich*, *Admiral* Raeder flew his flag on *Leipzig* between 22 and 26 March for the round voyage from Swinemünde, where on the 26th the cruiser fired a 21-gun salute for the *Führer* to mark the successful conclusion of the operation. *Kapitän zur See* Heinz Nordmann became the cruiser's fifth commander in April.

On 17 April, in company with the pocket-battleship *Deutschland*, the battleship *Gneisenau*, the 3rd Destroyer Division, the 6th and 7th U-Boat Flotillas, the tender *Erwin Wassner* and the oiler *Samland*, *Leipzig* sailed for the eastern Atlantic on the only large-scale German foreign naval exercise between the wars. Calls were made at Pontevedra and Corunna, the cruiser returning to Kiel on 18 May. In the remaining three months of peace *Leipzig* engaged in intensive exercises, mainly with *Nürnberg* and *Köln* but also with *Gneisenau* and destroyers in mid-August.

World War II

On 23 August a large force under *Vizeadmiral* Densch, BdA, received orders to take up blockading stations at the Baltic exits to deter Polish units from escaping to the West. As the German ships were not allowed to shoot, the blockade was ineffective and Densch was unable to prevent the passage of three Polish destroyers through the

Danish Narrows to Britain. In the first two weeks of September five Polish submarines also broke out, three being interned in Sweden and two arriving in Britain.

On 25 August *Leipzig*'s ship's company was informed of the situation by *Kapitän zur See* Nordmann and war watches were introduced on board ship. On 2 September *Leipzig* and other vessels of *Vizeadmiral* Densch's force transferred into the North Sea to lay a mine barrier which represented the seaward extension of the *Westwall* (or Siegfried Line). *Leipzig* worked throughout September out of Wilhelmshaven together with *Nürnberg* and the yacht *Grille*, joined on the 19th and 20th by the torpedo-boats *Seeadler* and *Wolf*. The operation was concluded on the 29th of the month and the cruiser repaired to the western Baltic, where she remained exercising until mid-November. On the 17th of that month, while in transit through the Holtenau Lock for Brunsbüttel, she collided with the gunnery training ship *Bremse*, but the damage was negligible. On 21 November, together with *Köln* and three destroyers, *Leipzig* escorted the battleships *Scharnhorst* and *Gneisenau* as far as the Skagerrak on their mission to roll up the Northern Patrol, and she remained on anti-contraband patrol until she escorted the battleships home on the 25th. On a number of occasions *Leipzig* and other cruisers had escorted homewards across the German Bight groups of German destroyers returning from minelaying missions along the British East Coast: all operations were successful until the fiasco of 13 December, when *Leipzig* and *Nürnberg* were torpedoed by HM Submarine *Salmon*.*

In his report, *Kapitän zur See* Nordmann stated that at 1125 that morning *Leipzig* was running at 28kt when a trail of bubbles was seen approaching the ship, and so close that the torpedo could not be avoided. He ordered hard to port, but almost at once a violent explosion occurred in the area of frame 89 just abaft the bulkhead between boiler rooms I and II and about 3–4m below the waterline. The boiler rooms flooded at once to the level of the armour grating, and here fourteen men drowned—two petty officers, one midshipman, nine stokers and two damage control ratings. The engine revolution counters showed that the port turbine stopped immediately, while the other slowed to a stop over the next fifteen minutes. The diesel-driven central propeller continued with revolutions for 15kt. The rudder obeyed the helm haltingly and would not remain where put but returned to midships. Manual helm was ordered. The torpedo hit on *Nürnberg* was observed, and a few minutes later she and *Köln* disappeared from sight on a westerly heading. Aboard *Leipzig* speed was cut to 10kt for fear of the damaged bulkhead giving way.

At 1225 Nordmann requested from the BdA a destroyer escort, but the fact that his radio location equipment and both gyro-compasses were not functioning was problematical. At 1315 a German reconnaissance aircraft arrived; fifteen minutes later, when *Nürnberg* and *Köln* reappeared, *Leipzig* took up close station on the latter for anti-aircraft protection, since her own flak was only partially operational; and at 1345 the group was joined at by the destroyers *Richard Beitzen* and *Bruno Heinemann*. At 1530 the BdA, *Konteradmiral* Lütjens, ordered *Leipzig* into Brunsbüttel.

At 0605 the following morning Nordmann signalled Group West: '*Leipzig* torpedo hit compartments VIII–IX, only one boiler working, difficulty steering manual rudder, two large lateral holes, one main longitudinal bulkhead torn open, request two powerful tugs at 1300 to assist progress at estuary.' At 0702 Group West replied, '*Leipzig* repair Wilhelmshaven.'

Leipzig proceeded until daybreak with the two destroyers leading and *Köln* astern. When the destroyers *Friedrich Ihn* and *Hermann Schoemann* arrived directly from the dockyard, *Köln* took station ahead of *Leipzig* with the four destroyers abeam. Between 0730 and 0815 the escort was further strengthened by *F 7*, *F 9*, six motor minesweepers of the 3rd R-Boat Flotilla, four boats of the 2nd Minesweeping Flotilla and several aircraft. At 0951 *Köln* was ordered by Group West to make for Wilhelmshaven at once and was detached at high speed with *Friedrich Ihn* and *Hermann Schoemann* as escorts. The anti-submarine screen now formed around *Leipzig* (see accompanying diagram).

At 1235 a violent explosion occurred in the escort vessel *F 9* about 800m ahead off the starboard bow. Assuming *F 9* to have been mined, Nordmann ordered 'Hard to port, stop diesel.' Almost immediately a track was reported on the starboard bow, the torpedo passing about 50m ahead. *Leipzig*'s diesel was restarted for full ahead. *F 9* foundered quickly on her port beam, the stern standing upright in the water for about twenty seconds before sinking. The motor minesweepers *R 36* and *R 38* picked up 34 survivors.

In his report, *Kapitän zur See* Nordmann was critical of the starboard escorts:

> Whereas it must be recognised that despite the unpleasant sea conditions for small boats the R-Flotillas zealously

---

* These events are covered more fully in the career details for *Nürnberg*.

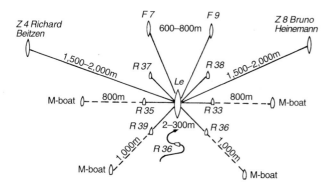

Above: Formation of the anti-submarine escort for *Leipzig*, 14 December 1939.

executed their zig-zags and needed no instruction, after the successful attack the escort vessels on the starboard side should have headed at once for the suspected shooting position of the submarine and dropped depth charges. Instead they scattered without making any attempt to come to grips with the attacker and left the endangered starboard side of *Leipzig* completely unprotected. To demoralise the submarine I ordered, on the ultra-short-wave band, 'Escort vessels starboard side drop depth charges.' This resulted in one depth charge being dropped by an unknown minesweeper. To summarise, it must be said that the escorts as anti-submarine escorts did not meet expectations. To judge by the track of bubbles, the submarine attacked from the starboard bow. As the cruiser had limited manoeuvrability, to turn along the ordered approach course for the Jade would have placed the cruiser favourably for an attack by the same submarine [HM Submarine *Ursula*]; by heading instead for the Elbe, *Leipzig* showed the submarine her stern. Therefore I headed for the Elbe. Because of the danger of the bulkhead giving way, speed was kept down to 10kt. It must be added that the escorts gave no further cause for complaint on the run in.

At 1429 the convoy passed Lightship H and at 1728 anchored in the roadstead at Brunsbüttel. The cruiser proceeded to Deutsche Werke shipyard at Kiel for repair.

On 8 January 1940 a BdA Court of Inquiry convened aboard the cruiser in the shipyard to investigate the circumstances surrounding the torpedoing. In his report *Admiral* Marschall, the Fleet Commanderr, came down heavily against Nordmann:

> . . . The anti-submarine escort formation chosen by *Leipzig* was unsuitable. The boats fitted with the valuable *S-Gerät* [hydrophone installation] could not use them, the formation was much too tight and, despite the number of available units, failed in their task. They amounted merely to 'a heap of escorts' and did not make the submarine's objective particularly difficult. The correct thing would have been an echelon formation with the hydrophone-equipped boats sailing about four to five kilometres ahead of the convoy, the destroyers and minesweepers building a line of defence about three kilometres off the damaged ship with only the R-boats as close escort, zig-zagging about 600 to 1,000m away. Furthermore, command of the escort should have been placed in the hands of the most senior Flotilla commander . . .
>
> . . . The measures taken by *Leipzig* and her escort after the 14 December torpedoing were inadequate. It was a serious tactical failure that the large number of escorts only managed to drop one depth charge. As the leading ship, *Leipzig* should have issued clear and unequivocal orders for engaging the enemy . . . it was essential to give the submarine alarm by all available methods (not merely, after a long delay, by a flag hoist 'Submarine to starboard'). There were no sirens or stars fired off, no indication of distance off or bearing of the attacking submarine, and no order to any escort in particular to carry out a depth-charge attack. Therefore I do not uphold the criticisms of the anti-submarine escort levelled by *Leipzig*'s commander, but I *must* censure the cruiser in that the measures taken in hand for the energetic use of the escort force were insufficient . . . I do not, by any means, underestimate the difficulties confronting the seriously damaged cruiser on the way home . . . and I accept that the commander's worries were so considerable that handling the escort force was rather thrust into the background. Accordingly, all the more proper and right it would have been for the commander to relieve himself of the burden of directing the anti-submarine force by delegating command to the most senior Flotilla commander present . . .

Later, *Admiral* Raeder, CinC *Kriegsmarine*, observed: 'The use of cruisers to escort destroyers or other light forces in the manner undertaken on 13 December 1939 proved unsuitable and inappropriate.'

The cruiser was decommissioned on 27 February. Orders came down that neither her top speed nor full battle-readiness need be restored, and a major refit scheduled for October 1940 was cancelled. *Leipzig* was relegated to training duties and the two boiler rooms devastated by the torpedo hit were rebuilt as cadets' dormitories with bunks. Externally, the after torpedo-tube mountings were unshipped and a degaussing system was fitted. The cruiser was recommissioned with a new permanent ship's company as a training vessel for the naval gunnery and torpedo schools under her sixth commander, *Kapitän zur See* Werner Stichling, at Danzig on 1 December 1940 following her first engine trials. During December she completed and fitted out, took aboard munitions, adjusted her radio installation, ran her acceptance voyage and calibrated her guns.

During the first half of 1941 the ship underwent a number minor refits, including the removal of the catapult installation and, from 4 March, the after torpedo tubes. These modifications alternated with the ship's training duties as part of the Torpedo School Flotilla. On 11 June *Leipzig*, five destroyers, two U-boats and a large air escort set off from Kiel, accompanying the heavy cruiser *Lützow* (ex *Deutschland*) as far as Norway on the first stage of her commerce-raiding voyage to the Indian Ocean code-named Operation 'Sommerreise'. After the naval escort had put into Oslo Fjord, *Lützow* continued alone, but she was torpedoed by an aircraft off Egersund and had to abandon her mission. On 7 July *Leipzig* returned to Germany led by the *Sperrbrecher Belgrad*. On her arrival at Travemünde she was inspected by *Konteradmiral* Thiele, Chief of Staff to the Fleet. The cruiser lay at Copenhagen from 12 August to 1 September and after degaussing tests at Travemünde sailed in company with *Nürnberg* to Swinemünde on 21 September. *Leipzig* was by now virtually battle-ready, and on the 24th she arrived at Libau for the 'Weststurm I' and 'II' operations, in which, with *Emden*, three torpedo-boats and E-boats she formed South Group of the so-called Baltic Fleet. Between 25 and 27 September South Group bombarded Soviet land targets and artillery positions on the Sworbe peninsula in support of the German troop landings on the Estonian island of Ösel. On the 27th she avoided torpedoes from the Russian submarine *SC-317* and attacks by Russian MTBs.* On her return to Kiel the cruiser entered Deutsche Werke until 20 October, during which time she spent eight days in drydock. Between 22 October and 11 November she worked out of Gotenhafen, assisting the heavy cruiser *Admiral Scheer* to work up. Gunnery and torpedo training exercises then continued until the year's end.

Throughout 1942 *Leipzig* was engaged in training duties and exercises in the central Baltic. On 14 April she was appointed flagship of *Konteradmiral* Litzmann, Commander Fleet Training Ships. New 15cm gun barrels were fitted at Stettin between 15 April and 7 May. At the end of the year the cruiser entered drydock at Deutsche Werke, Libau, where she remained until 13 January 1943, not leaving the yards until 15 February. During the period her seventh commander, *Kapitän zur See* Friedrich-Traugott Schmidt, was aboard from August to September 1942, when the ship's eighth commander, *Kapitän zur See* Waldemar Winther, took over until February 1943.

Leipzig was included in the general decommissioning of heavy units deprecated as 'worthless and useless' by Hitler following the Barents Sea fiasco of 30 December 1942, and her ensign was hauled down at Libau on 4 March 1943. In the deteriorating military situation work existed even for a worn-down cruiser, however, and after a new permanent ship's company had been mustered *Leipzig* was recommissioned on 1 August and began working up at once. On 10 August a potentially serious fire in boiler room III was swiftly extinguished. Steaming, flak exercises and shipyard trials were followed by a brief period in drydock to repair the port propeller on 7 September. Training duties resumed in the Bay of Danzig with courses for helmsmen, engineering and navigation cadets.

Kapitän zur See Walter Hülsemann became the cruiser's ninth commander in October. During the air raid on Gotenhafen on 9 October *Leipzig* joined in the air defence with her flak batteries. In refits during the year the two forward torpedo tube mountings were landed and an FuMO 25 radar aerial was fitted on the battlemast. Between 15 and 25 December the main gun barrels were unshipped at Gotenhafen, and the cruiser was laid up in the port from 20 December until 5 January 1944 for the Christmas period. On Christmas Day the ship's pinnace helped in the rescue operations for the crew of *Sperrbrecher 30*.

During January 1944 *Leipzig* underwent an overhaul at Deutsche Werke, Gotenhafen, which included the refitting of the new 15cm main gun barrels. Training courses continued aboard whilst in the shipyard and working up. At Swinemünde *Vizeadmiral* Meendsen-Bohlken, Fleet Commander, inspected the battle-readiness of the ship on 23 August. *Kapitän zur See* Heinrich Spörel became the ship's tenth commander on 26 August. After an outbreak of cerebrospinal meningitis was confirmed at Swinemünde on 30 August, the cruiser went into quarantine at Misdroy until 12 September but suffered two shipboard deaths from the disease. On 15 September convoy exercises were held with *Admiral Scheer*, and on the 26th of the month *Leipzig* ran several escorts for troop transports between Gotenhafen and Swinemünde. On the 30th, led by three minesweepers, she sailed for Hela with the U-boat tender *Tsingtau* and a U-boat astern and on 4 October exercised off the port with *Admiral Hipper*, *Köln* and the old battleship *Schlesien*, proceeding in convoy for the Schichau shipyard at Danzig. Between 9 and 14 October *Leipzig*

---

* See the footnote concerning this action in the career details for *Emden*.

was anchored at Gotenhafen, where the disastrous chain of events culminating in the collision with the heavy cruiser *Prinz Eugen* on 15 October had their inception, as described in a very clear manner in *Kapitän zur See* Spörel's immediate accident report:

When I took command of *Leipzig* on 26 August 1944 the general war situation seemed grave. The collapse on the Eastern Front was evident. The repercussions in the *Wehrmacht* following the events of 20 July 1944 [the date of the Bomb Plot] were making themselves felt. The crippling of the *Kriegsmarine*, particularly that of the U-boat arm, was having an unfavourable effect on morale at all levels.

I soon discovered that the mood aboard ship was subdued and discontented. This was partly due to a completely unsatisfactory battle-readiness inspection on 20 August which the Fleet Commander had ordered to be repeated. The causes behind this failure were probably to be found in the fact that since the torpedoing of 13 December 1939 the ship had spent two long periods out of commission, she had only been repaired where absolutely necessary, and the ship's company had, with few exceptions, been drawn from the Personnel Reserve on the last commissioning (1 August 1943) and was completely disorganised. Some of the officers came from Coastal Artillery and had never been aboard a ship; others had been discarded for incompetence or as misfits and landed. By way of example, my Executive Officer (IO) had been the commanding officer of a minesweeping flotilla relieved of command because of his inability to handle men. The Navigation Officer (NO) was a former harbour pilot at Danzig and knew nothing about warships. He had survived an attempt by my predecessor to dismiss him. Another of my officers was a *Kapitänleutnant* who had not come up to standard as a U-boat watchkeeping officer. Therefore I had few officers upon whom I could rely unconditionally. Excepted from this statement are the Chief Engineer, *Korvettenkapitän* Grundmann; the No 1 Gunnery Officer, *Kapitänleutnant* Plass; the Wireless Officer, *Kapitänleutnant* König; and *Leutnant zur See* Boldemann. Most of the warrant officers and knowledgable mates were good, although only a few had any battle experience. With such a corps of officers and NCOs it was soon obvious that it would be very difficult to get a lame ship battleworthy or even carry out a simple operation successfully.

The other ranks were made up of 80 per cent cadets and were very good. This encouraged me to really come to grips with the problem. Besides the Gunnery Officer, Wireless Officer and myself, no officer had shipboard battle experience. This meant that I had to start from the beginning—something of an advantage, as it subsequently proved. Through constant contact with the crew, including addresses over the ship's loudspeakers, I succeeded in gaining their confidence, giving them pride in their ship,

making her into a fighting unit and to bolstering their self-confidence. Thus after six weeks *Leipzig* passed the repeat battle-readiness inspection to the satisfaction of the Fleet Commander, although the Navigation Officer failed so completely that the Admiral ordered me to submit a drafting request on his behalf.

On 11 October 1944 the cruiser was in Danzig shipyard for a brief refit when I received bad news from home and obtained compassionate leave to visit Torgau hospital until 15 October. I made sure that my IO and ADC knew how to contact me in Torgau should the need arise. On my arrival at Torgau I reported to the military commander and called in every day of my leave to see if there were any messages for me. I left there on 14 October. My train connection had been bombed at Erfurt so I had to take a detour via Bromberg and got to Danzig seven hours late on the 15th. One of my officers met me on the platform with a telex containing orders for *Leipzig* to sail at 1500 that day to load mines at Swinemünde. We had to travel on to Gotenhafen, where the ship had berthed at midday. When I got there I was met by *Korvettenkapitän* Kopp, Admiral Staff Officer, who told me that Fleet Command had made several enquiries to establish why *Leipzig* had not confirmed her sailing orders. I explained my own misfortunes and, as he had been appointed my new Navigation Officer, asked why he had not taken up his duties aboard. He replied that he had been ordered to wait until his own relief arrived from Norway. Until then I would have to sail with the present Navigation Officer. There was nothing I could do about this, but I asked Kopp to inform his commanding officer that I could not possibly carry out a minelaying operation without a competent navigator.

My Chief Engineer was waiting at Training Command to tell me that the IO had ordered him not to raise steam. I Morsed the order to the ship at once and we then boarded. I learned, to my consternation, that the sailing order had been received on 12 October. The IO and ADC had not considered it important enough to contact me at Torgau because they expected me back in the morning of the 15th.

Fleet Command was pressing us to sail, and so there was no time to go through the usual departure routine, check mine or submarine warnings nor find out the general war situation in the Baltic, and I was still getting changed when *Leipzig* weighed anchor at 1745. We took station behind a *Sperrbrecher* and left Gotenhafen with the IO in charge on the bridge. As there was not yet sufficient pressure in the boilers for turbine drive, the ship was motoring on her central propeller, driven by the cruise diesel. I ordered the ship closed up at war stations, and when I came on the bridge the Wireless Officer handed me a signal warning that the heavy cruiser *Prinz Eugen*, returning from Memel, would be entering Gotenhafen at about 2000. Standing orders stated that the second copy of a signal had to be given simultaneously to the NO on the bridge and then passed on by him to the IO. Unfortunately, the second copy of this signal was intercepted by the IO and neither the NO nor the officer of the watch saw it. Thus they knew nothing about *Prinz Eugen*. The Wireless Officer referred to some earlier signals, of which a German U-boat's report of a torpedo track off Hela concerned me most. I went out on the bridge and mentioned it to the NO. It was 1942 and we were bearing 293 degrees off the Hela light. At that moment the engine room reported 'Steam up in all boilers and outer propellers ready to couple in.' At the same time the signal deck reported that the *Sperr-brecher* was turning back. I ordered the officer of the watch to stop the diesel. The WO asked the NO on what side he should pass the mid-channel buoy dividing swept channel No 76 into westbound (port) and eastbound (starboard) lanes. We were making for Swinemünde, which was to our west. The NO said, 'It doesn't matter.' I contradicted him and pointed out, 'You are obliged to pass to port of it but now it is too late. Go round it on the starboard side and bring the ship to a stop there.' I thought it was outrageous that a *Kapitänleutnant* who had served as a WO for years and must have known these waters better than I from his U-boat service knew nothing about simple navigation. I took over command, and after passing the buoy stopped the ship after ascertaining from observations of the buoy that there was no tidal stream running. The wind was south-south-east, Force 1–2, with variable visibility and mist patches. I expected the stop to last about ten minutes. While waiting for the outer propellers to be coupled in I discussed with the NO what measures should be taken to reduce the danger of submarine attack in the swept channel, since we were prohibited from zigzagging while in it. I came to the conclusion that in waters with irregular tidal flow a ship should proceed at varying speeds and instructed the NO to prepare his course adjustments, which he would then pass in a series of orders to the WO from the charthouse. The NO said that he did not know how to do this. I had no choice but to go to the charthouse and give the instruction to a competent warrant officer coxswain.

At 1958 the completion of the coupling-in was reported to me via the voicetube. I ordered the cruiser to 15kt and extinguished the running lights on account of the submarine danger. As the ship was straddling the mid-channel line I pointed the bow an extra 3 degrees to starboard.*

The War Diary entry at 2001 states laconically: 'Heavy cruiser *Prinz Eugen* collided into compartment X, port side, at angle of 35 degrees. Location of incident: 54° 35.3′ N 18° 54.2′ E.' The Explanatory Notes to the *Leipzig* War Diary record:

At 1958 ship got under way with orders for 15kt on course 90°, which meant she was not athwart the channel. *Prinz Eugen* had navigation lanterns set dimly and in the conditions [of dark and mist] they could not be seen. It was thus not possible to judge her angle of approach. Only her masthead steaming lights were visible. Accordingly, the *Leipzig* WO acted correctly by attempting to avoid the steaming lights dead ahead by turning hard to starboard. Aboard *Prinz Eugen* the officers were taken by surprise when *Leipzig*'s navigation lanterns came on suddenly. *Prinz Eugen* was making 20kt, which was excessive for the swept channel; *Leipzig* ran foul of her at about 9kt. As soon as she saw the lanterns, *Prinz Eugen* set her Night Signal Apparatus to three red and three white alternating lights, which means 'My engines are full astern.' Having regard to the short distance involved, the effect of reversing engines was negligible.

The two ships, dovetailed together, were finally wrenched apart at 1400 on 16 October. *Prinz Eugen*'s bows had carved into *Leipzig* between the battlemast and the funnel almost to the centreline, and held the light cruiser fast between her centre keel plate and upper deck 'rather like a shark with its prey,' as *Fregattenkapitän* Schmalenbach, *Prinz Eugen*'s Gunnery Officer, described it. For a while much of *Leipzig*'s weight was resting on *Prinz Eugen*'s central keel plates and was not reduced until the heavy cruiser was trimmed deep. The bow had bored into boiler room III, tearing away the bulkhead between boiler rooms II and III. The ship being closed up at war stations prevented a worse catastrophe. As it was, the collision claimed 19 dead and 30 injured aboard *Leipzig*.

Leipzig was brought into Gotenhafen's Basin V with tug assistance but could not dock and so went into the 70,000-tonne floating dock instead, where she remained until 30 December. A proper repair was out of the question, and the crew set to making the ship seaworthy using improvised tools and materials. The damage was so serious, however, that the cruiser was finally condemned to be used a training hulk for cadets. Because of the now daily air raids she limped regularly to different spots about

---

* Despite Spörel's criticism of his officers, and the absence of a map showing the swept channel, his seems to have been the fatal error. The cruiser's War Diary does not assert that *Leipzig* was in the correct channel; it merely states that the cruiser was not at right angles across the waterway. Spörel states that, as his ship was straddling the line between the port and starboard channels, he increased her heading to *starboard* by an extra 3 degrees, thus driving her forward at a slight angle into the wrong channel as she worked up to 15kt in mist and fog. What possessed him to make the error he does not explain, and nobody on the bridge questioned his order in the three minutes remaining before *Prinz Eugen* loomed out of the mist in her correct channel, heading for *Leipzig* at 20kt.—G.B.

164

the harbour. Spörel left the cruiser in November 1944 and the IO, *Korvettenkapitän* Hagen Küster, supervised the ship's business until January 1944.

On 2 February 1945 *Korvettenkapitän* Walter Bach became *Leipzig*'s eleventh and last commander. Because of the deteriorating military situation in the East, instructions had been issued to get the cruiser seaworthy at all costs. As the shipyard had virtually ceased to function, a blind eye was turned to any means of improvisation, and measures included expropriation; for example, the origins of a powerful diesel motor and several generators were never established. On 13 February *Leipzig* moved from Basin V to Basin I under her own power. On 16 February the guns were exercised with two rounds per barrel. From 17 February to 4 March the ship worked up intensively and cared for many refugees.

On 9 March, at 16km distant, the Russians were within range of *Leipzig*'s 15cm guns and 'C' turret fired 53 rounds, including 22 at assembly areas near Tuchum. The Russians targeted *Leipzig*, forcing her to change her position frequently. Between 14 and 24 March, from various locations within the port of Gotenhafen or at sea beyond the range of Russian artillery, *Leipzig* fired 920 15cm shells, causing massive damage, particularly to enemy artillery. On 17 March the 7th Panzer Division signalled, 'We thank you for your outstanding shooting.' The ship's flak was very successful and made two confirmed kills of Russian aircraft. Decorations were awarded to crew members by *Vizeadmiral* Rogge on 23 March.

By 24 March there was no more 15cm ammunition to be had and *Leipzig* moved to Hela to embark about 500 refugees and Army wounded before weighing anchor at about

1930 for the long and dangerous voyage westwards. She was accompanied by six merchant vessels and a few small escorts and could make 6kt through waters patrolled by Soviet submarines and below skies across which the enemy air forces had total air supremacy. On the first night submarines were seen visually and also detected by hydrophone. A torpedo was avoided by a sharp turn to starboard. Russian reconnaissance aircraft flew overhead. The first air attack arrived on the 26th when six Soviet torpedo aircraft came in from astern. While the flak put up a curtain of fire, the stern was angled towards whichever aircraft seemed to be making a run. This was done in order to reduce the ship's profile. Once within range of the light flak, the aircraft always turned away. Although many submarine alarms were probably false, on the night of 27 March, at the entrance to the swept channel, a Soviet submarine made an attack while Russian aircraft circled overhead. A merchant vessel was slightly damaged by the aircraft and a torpedo crossed the *Leipzig*'s wash about 20m astern. Weather favourable to the German convoy—fog and mist—began to close in, and on the 29th the cruiser moored at Apenrade.

Leipzig remained in the Danish port with her ship's company until 30 June 1945, when she joined a British escort for Wilhelmshaven. Here she was decommissioned on 20 December 1945. Because of her desolate condition she was not wanted by any of the victorious powers and was found employment at Wilhelmshaven as an accommodation hulk for minesweeper crews. On 9 July 1946 three tugs towed her to the Skagerrak, where on the 20th she was destroyed by scuttling charges at 57° 53′ N 6° 13′ E, south-west of Farsund.

Right: The World War I light cruiser *Leipzig*, 3,276 tons, was launched at AG Weser, Bremen, on 21 March 1905 and entered service with the Fleet on 20 April 1906. At the outbreak of war she was attached to the Far East Cruiser Squadron based on Tsingtau, China. On 1 November she took a minor part in the Battle of Coronel off the Chilean coast, obtaining a hit on the light cruiser *Glasgow* before losing contact in the darkness. On 8 December 1914, in the Battle of the Falkland Islands, *Leipzig* fought on for more than three hours, obtaining a number of hits on both enemy ships, until her ammunition was exhausted. She refused to strike her flag and was bombarded until she signalled her hopeless plight an hour later, finally sinking at 2122, six hours after battle commenced. *Cornwall* rescued her fifteen survivors, including six officers. Armament: 10 × 10.5cm guns, two torpedo tubes. Machinery: steam piston engines coupled to turbines supplied by ten coal-fired watertube boilers, speed 22kt. Dimensions: 110.6 × 13.3 × 5.6m. Complement: 14 officers and up to 287

men. The photograph shows a flag-bedecked *Leipzig* at a jetty in an east Asian port. The light cruiser *Leipzig* (iii) was launched at AG Weser, Bremen, on 28 January 1918 but was incomplete when scrapped in 1921 under the Armistice provisions. Her details were generally as for *Königsberg* (ii).

Left, upper: *Leipzig* at launch. After the naming ceremony, the bow shield is unveiled and the canvas sheet bearing the ship's name is unfurled.

Left, lower: Slowly, then increasingly quickly, the hull slides down to the water. To the left is *Hannover*, one of the old pre-dreadnoughts.

Above: The cruiser fitting out. 'B' and 'C' turrets are already shipped, and the long deckhouse is still unroofed to permit the delivery of material to the lower decks.

Right: The ship, near to completion, in drydock for a thorough inspection and a final coat of paint below the waterline.

167

Left, upper: Wilhelmshaven Navy Yard from the air, 28 August 1931. In Drydock I are the fishery protection vessels *Elbe* and *Weser*; in Drydock V is the gunnery target ship *Zähringen*; along the south quay opposite are the old torpedo-boats *G 8* and *G 10*; in Drydock VI are minesweepers; before Drydocks IV to VI are modern torpedo-boats; and on Slipway 1 can be seen the pocket-battleship *Admiral Scheer* under construction. *Leipzig* is seen across the ways.

Left, lower: *Leipzig* photographed before entering service.

Right: The new cruiser was commissioned ceremonially on 8 October 1931. The photograph shows the raising of the naval ensign. The large tripod frame belongs to the shipboard floating crane.

Below: *Leipzig* proceeding to Entrance III, 4 November 1931, with an admiral's flag fluttering at the foretop pole.

Above: *Leipzig* under tow through the harbour canal at Wilhelmshaven Navy Yard, 14 April 1932. Beyond her stern is the *Langer Heinrich* floating crane; in the left background is the old battleship *Hannover*.

Below: *Leipzig* at the Alaska moorings (today Nordhafen), 1 June 1936; to her right lies the old battleship *Schleswig-Holstein*. The barracks date from the *Kaiser*'s time. The large buildings are the Harbour Barracks and Shipyard Barracks, the smaller block the later Graf Spee Barracks.

Opposite, top left: The main fire control of the cruiser was located in the foretop. The red pennant indicates that the cruiser is engaged in firing practice.

Opposite, top right: The single funnel with aerial booms mounted at the rear of the mantle. Searchlight positions are fitted either side of the funnel. In the foreground is a davit.

Opposite, lower: A stern view of *Leipzig* in the lock chamber in 1934. The ship's company is mustered on the quarterdeck.

Left, top: *Leipzig* in the fitting-out basin at Wilhelmshaven. At the Catering Office Quay is the pre-dreadnought battleship *Schleswig-Holstein*.

Left, centre: *Leipzig* at sea.

Left, bottom: *Leipzig* entering the Baltic port of Swinemünde. Notice the similarity of the bridge structure, tubular battlemast and night fire control centre to those of the cruiser *Königsberg* and the pocket-battleship *Deutschland*.

Right: A look aft from the foretop, affording a good view of the after turrets and boat stations. Ship's boats always approach alongside from astern and are stowed aboard bow-forward. Notice also the searchlight positions. Alongside is *T 155*, one of the old Imperial Navy torpedo-boats.

Above: In July 1934 *Reichsmarine* warships visited a British port for the first time since the Great War. This photograph shows *Leipzig* entering Portsmouth.

Left: A view of the cruiser at Portsmouth: beyond her is *Königsberg*, flying the pennant of the BdA.

Below: *Leipzig* moored at Kiel. Fluttering from the signal halyards of the battlemast is 'the laundry'.

Right, upper: Each year the *Reichsmarine* held a rowing race known in Navy circles as the '*Kutterrees*' ('Cutter Madness') at Kieler Förde, when most units entered at least one boat. The photograph shows *Leipzig* being passed by numerous competing cutters during one of the races.

Right, lower: The light cruiser *Emden* in October 1937 at the Gazelle Bridge (later renamed Bonte Quay), Wilhelmshaven, preparing to leave on a long foreign cruise. *Leipzig*'s crew parade in salute at the starboard rail of their ship.

Above: *Leipzig* at Kiel. Notice the new pole mast fixed to the funnel mantle, replacing the previous booms.

Left: *Leipzig* during Fleet gunnery exercises in 1938, her flak guns manned and torpedo tubes trained abeam ready to fire. The new-issue blue side cap is being worn by crew members for the first time.

Right, top: *Leipzig* in the Wilhelmshaven roadstead between Fleet manoeuvres on 19 June 1938. Her new shipboard crane and Heinkel 60 floatplane on the catapult between battlemast and funnel are seen for the first time. During the Spanish Civil War the cruiser ran trials with the American single-float Vought Corsair.

Right, centre: *Leipzig* during a refuelling drill known as 'towed and being towed'. Note the taut hawser at the bow.

Right, bottom: At Kiel. A pinnace approaching from astern steers for the accommodation ladder amidships, and a second pinnace is made fast to the boom forward. *Leipzig*'s company is paraded at the port rail and the *Reich* War Flag flies at the foretop.

Left: A gunnery mechanic on board the cruiser *Köln* just happened to be on deck with his camera as smoke began to envelop *Leipzig* following the torpedo hit obtained on her by the British submarine *Salmon* on 13 December 1939.
Below: *Leipzig* wearing camouflage in the Baltic, 1941.
Right: *Leipzig* was never fully operational again following the torpedoing of 13 December 1939, and in October 1944, in the Baltic, she was rammed amidships in fog by the heavy cruiser *Prinz Eugen*. These photographs show the two ships dovetailed together. Note the various radar antennas on the cruiser's battlemast.

Above: Many hours passed before the two cruisers could be separated. In this photograph *Prinz Eugen* is being dragged clear by the stern. Alongside *Leipzig* is a torpedo-boat, while a salvage tug awaits orders in the background.

Left: The military funeral for the *Leipzig* crewmen killed in the collision with *Prinz Eugen*.

Left: *Leipzig* at one of her berths at Gotenhafen, March 1945.
Below: 'B' and 'C' turrets bombard Soviet land positions.

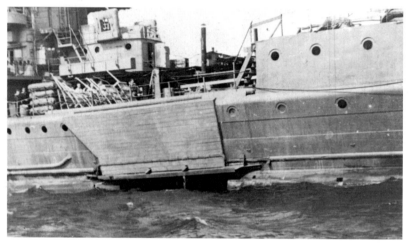

Left, top: On 25 March 1945 *Leipzig* left Hela at her top speed of 6kt with 500 refugees aboard. In the ensuing three-day voyage she navigated her way across the mine-infested Baltic, surviving Soviet air and submarine attack, to put in at Apenrade in Denmark unscathed. This photograph, taken from the bridge platform, shows the cruiser's slight list to port on arrival.

Left, centre: *Leipzig* remained at Apenrade until the capitulation. This is the midships site of the ramming, the gap sealed temporarily with planking, boards and other materials.

Left, bottom: In mid-May 1945 *Leipzig* was brought to Wilhelmshaven pending a decision as to her fate. In this photograph, taken on 9 July 1946, she is being towed from the Bonte Quay past the Kaiser Wilhelm Bridge and the old southern centre of the shipyard.

Right, upper: It is doubtful from these last photographs—which show the hull riding relatively high in the water—that the cruiser was at this time loaded with gas shells and other unwanted munitions prior to being scuttled.

Right, lower: Three tugs, including *Enak* and *Heros*, edge the cruiser to the quayside at Entrance III (Tirpitz Lock) to make fast for the last time. Notice, on the quarterdeck, the two 2cm flak guns with splinter shielding.

Below: A stern view of *Leipzig* and the tug *D 2* in the lock chamber.

Far left: The lock gate open, *Leipzig* is towed stern-first into the chamber.

Left: *Leipzig* anchored at the location where she is to be scuttled. Notice the taut chain of the port anchor. Astern is the tug bringing the demolition party.

Left, lower: *Leipzig* seen from abeam, starboard side, with tug astern.

Right, top: Having re-embarked the demolition squad, the tug makes off to a safe distance.

Right, centre and bottom: Concealed within a massive billow of smoke as the scuttling charges explode, the cruiser *Leipzig* meets her end, 20 July 1946.

Nürnberg

The building contract for Cruiser 'F' (Replacement *Nymphe*) was lodged with Deutsche Werft, Kiel, on 16 March 1933 under Yard Number 234, the first keel sections being laid on 4 November that year. *Nürnberg* was launched on 8 December 1934, the twentieth anniversary of the sinking of the light cruiser *Nürnberg* (i) during the Battle of the Falkland Islands. *Bürgermeister* Niebel of Nuremberg delivered the baptismal speech, and *Frau* Lehfeldt, daughter of *Fregattenkapitän* von Schönberg, commander of *Nürnberg* (i), named the ship. *Kapitän zur See* Hubert Schmundt commissioned the cruiser on 2 November 1935 and her trials and working-up took place over the ensuing months.

Prewar Service

On 9 April *Nürnberg* was appointed flagship of *Konteradmiral* Boehm, BdA (*Befehlshaber der Aufklärungsstreitkräfte*, Commander Naval Scouting Forces). On 14 May she left for Atlantic exercises with *Leipzig* and *Köln*, visiting Tenerife and Lisbon before returning to Kiel on 8 May. On the occasion of the dedication of the Naval Memorial at Laboe, *Nürnberg* lay at Kiel between 28 May and 1 June and formed part of the naval review.

Between 3 and 19 June BdA manoeuvres were held in the Baltic with *Köln*, *Leipzig*, a torpedo-boat flotilla and minesweepers. On the 6th and 7th the group put into Swinemünde, and while off Skagen from 12 to 14 June the CinC, *Admiral* Raeder, came aboard from the state yacht *Grille*. The cruiser was in the yards throughout July 1936, the month when civil war broke out in Spain.

On 19 August a German naval force consisting of the pocket-battleship *Admiral Graf Spee*, the light cruisers *Nürnberg* (flagship BdA), *Leipzig* and four torpedo-boats sailed for Spanish waters to relieve *Konteradmiral* Karls, BdSp (*Befehlshaber der Spanienstreitkräfte*, Commander of Naval Forces Spain). After calls at Barcelona and Alicante, *Nürnberg* relieved *Köln* off Cadiz. The squadron returned on 9 October to Kiel, where *Kapitän zur See* Theodor-Heinrich Riedel became *Nürnberg*'s second commander.

In November the cruiser proceeded to Arosa Bay, and she remained in Spanish waters until 16 December, when she returned to Germany with *Admiral Scheer* and the 3rd Torpedo-Boat Flotilla.

During January and February 1937 the BdA hoisted his command flag aboard *Admiral Scheer* while *Nürnberg* spent two months having a scheduled refit followed by sea trials and crew training. On 24 April the cruiser departed to patrol off Cadiz, *Konteradmiral* Boehm, BdA, re-embarking on the 29th. *Nürnberg* berthed at Kiel on 19 May. Late that month *Nürnberg* and *Karlsruhe* engaged in exercises with U-boats and *Luftwaffe* units, and in June in Fleet manoeuvres. On 17 June *Nürnberg* sailed with *Admiral Graf Spee* and the 4th T-Boat Flotilla on a round trip to relieve *Admiral Scheer* and *Leipzig* off Lagos, Portugal (the latter ships having been instructed to withdraw on account of unexplained submarine torpedo attacks). At the beginning of August the squadron to which *Nürnberg* was attached also returned to Germany.

In September the one great *Wehrmacht* exercise was held. At sea the pocket-battleships *Deutschland* and *Admiral Graf Spee*, the cruisers *Nürnberg*, *Karlsruhe* and *Leipzig*, destroyers, torpedo-boats and other units were in the North Sea (6th–16th) and Baltic (17th–25th). On the 27th *Nürnberg* entered Deutsche Werke at Kiel for a refit which lasted until 20 November. Her third commander, *Kapitän zur See* Walter Krastel, took over in October. Radio installation and tuning work, trials and a gunnery exercise off Kiel preceded another refit which took place from 18 December.

From 4 to 18 January 1938 the cruiser carried out gunnery practice with the *Luftwaffe* and other exercises, extended into March. *Nürnberg* took part in the Fleet Display at Swinemünde on 13 March before engaging in BdA exercises from the 14th to the 23rd; a battle-readiness inspection was carried out by the BdA on the 24th and 25th. At the end of March *Nürnberg* entered the yards for an refit lasting into June, and she sailed for Norway on the 29th for a overseas training cruise, visiting Romsdal Fjord and Andalsnes. On 13 and 14 July torpedo practice was held in Eckernförder Bay, and from 19 to 27 July a torpedo exercise was mounted in Lübeck Bay with the three pocket-battleships, the old battleship *Schleswig-Holstein*, the cruisers *Köln* and *Leipzig*, destroyers, torpedo-boats and other vessels.

From 8 August *Nürnberg*, *Admiral Scheer*, *Admiral Graf Spee*, *Leipzig*, *Köln* and the 2nd Destroyer Division carried out drill with live ammunition in the central Baltic. On the 22nd *Nürnberg* took part in the Naval Review before Hitler and the Hungarian Regent Admiral Horthy to mark the launching of the heavy cruiser *Prinz Eugen*. Between 23 August and 3 September the cruiser exercised with KdF ('Strength Through Joy') liners in the Baltic and North Sea, and from the 14th to the 17th of the month engaged in Fleet manoeuvres.

During November there were two changes of command: *Kapitän zur See* Heinz Degenhardt was appointed for a short period before *Kapitän zur See* Otto Klüber took over as the cruiser's fifth commander. On 8 December *Nürnberg* visited Kiel to celebrate the launch of the aircraft carrier *Graf Zeppelin*, and on the 15th the cruiser ran speed trials over the measured mile in the Bay of Danzig before spending Christmas at moorings at Kiel.

From 5 January 1939 *Nürnberg* exercised alone in the Baltic. On 4 February she left Swinemünde for Hamburg, where with *Admiral Scheer* and torpedo-boats she represented the Fleet at the launching of the battleship *Bismarck*. On her return to Kiel there followed a brief lay-up in the yards before the March BdA exercises. For the reincorporation of Memel into the *Reich*, *Nürnberg* sailed with the three pocket-battleships, *Leipzig*, *Köln*, eight destroyers and nine torpedo-boats on the two-day mission commencing on 23 March, Hitler having embarked aboard *Deutschland*. After visiting Memel from the 22nd to the 24th, *Nürnberg* cruised in the Baltic for three days and ran machinery trials over the measured mile at Pillau. From 6 to 10 May she called in at Göteborg in Sweden and Geiranger Fjord, Norway. *Vizeadmiral* Densch, BdA, inspected the ship on 17 May. Following flak and gunnery practice with live ammunition on 5 June, the remainder of the month was spent in a large-scale Fleet exercise with *Gneisenau*, *Admiral Scheer*, *Admiral Graf Spee*, *Leipzig*, *Köln*, destroyers, minesweepers, escorts and U-boats, followed by a gunnery practice with the two light cruisers alone and a short engine overhaul. On 1 July *Nürnberg* was at Bremen for the launch of the heavy cruiser *Lützow*, after which she exercised with Fleet units until mid-August.

World War II

At the end of August 1939 *Konteradmiral* Densch, with *Nürnberg* as flagship, spread a task force of 38 warships, including *Leipzig*, *Köln*, destroyers, torpedo-boats and numerous support vessels, across the western and central Baltic to prevent the escape of Polish naval units. On 2 September, when it was obvious that 'the bird had flown', she entered the North Sea and on the 3rd, in company with *Leipzig*, destroyers and torpedo-boats, began work mining the German Bight from the Dutch coast to the Skagerrak so as to extend the defensive *Westwall* seawards. On 4 and 5 September the state yacht *Grille* and more destroyers and torpedo-boats joined the force. The operation, based at Wilhelmshaven, continued until 20 September, when *Nürnberg* returned to the Baltic.

On 1 and 2 November *Nürnberg* and *Leipzig* practised meeting at sea, after which the former went into the yards for a short refit; *Konteradmiral* Lütjens had replaced Densch as BdA on 21 October, and as soon as *Nürnberg* rejoined the Fleet on 9 November he hoisted his flag to her foretop and headed for the North Sea. On 12 November *Nürnberg*, *Köln* and six torpedo-boats came out from behind the *Westwall* minefield to meet six destroyers returning from a minelaying sortie in the Thames estuary—a mission repeated on 17 November. A similar operation on 12 December ended in a disastrous fiasco.

Since a light cruiser rates more highly than a destroyer, the logic of using light cruisers to protect destroyers must first be explained. As stated by Lütjens in his report, although the proper escort for a destroyer is a torpedo-boat, both T-boat flotillas were in the shipyard for refit or engine overhaul respectively; only *Seeadler* and *Jaguar* were operational, and these were in the Baltic. The only destroyers operational in the whole Fleet were the five engaged in the minelaying, although it was 'hoped' that two more could be repaired in time. *Admiral* Marschall, Fleet CinC, stated in his report that although it was clear to him from the outset of this operation that the presence of British submarines in the North Sea presented a threat to the cruisers, the risk was justified on the following grounds:

(a) Until then British submarines had had no success;

(b) it was preferable to have a cruiser torpedoed now and again rather than that smaller active-duty units should gain the impression that cruisers just lay at anchor while smaller units were thrown into action against all manner of superior forces without any support; and

(c) the morale of crews suffers severely in the long run if they are always clear to sail but never receive orders to do so.

Thus the drawbacks of this type of operation had to be accepted, there being no successful warfare without risk.

Five destroyers operating in two groups succeeded in laying 240 mines off the Tyne during the night of 12 December. They then headed for the rendezvous with the three cruisers. After *Bruno Heinemann* had beaten off three British aircraft at about 1030 the following morning, she met up with the flag destroyer *Hermann Künne* and *Friedrich Ihn*, *Richard Beitzen* and *Erich Steinbrinck*. These five destroyers were sighted by German reconnaissance aircraft at about this time in Grid Square 3741 on a heading to the north-east, the three German cruisers with which they were to rendezvous being north of them and below the horizon.

At 1730 the previous evening *Nürnberg*, *Leipzig* and *Köln* had left Schillig Roads for the north-west corner of the mine barrage. *Vizeadmiral* Lütjens had orders from Naval Command West to rendezvous there with the five returning destroyers at about 1130 next morning. At 0837 on 13 December *Leipzig*'s and *Nürnberg*'s aircraft were catapulted off to fly anti-submarine escort while the cruisers steered various courses in the formation of a triangle with 1,200m long sides. Wind was variable, Force 2–3, sea state 2, cloudy but with good visibility.

At about the time when the five destroyers had met up and were about 60 miles south of the cruisers, the cruisers' aircraft were released to the island of Sylt. It had been arranged that two Heinkel 115 floatplanes would replace them, but these did not arrive over the cruisers until 1125, about fifty minutes later.

At 1040 a suspicious steamer was sighted by the cruisers. The *Köln* War Diary states that 'At first the steamer seemed to be heading east, but as we approached she was heading west. It could not be determined if she was attempting to disguise her movements. With reference to the submarine attack shortly after, the suspicion of co-operation with the British submarine arises.'

The War Diary also recorded that 'The letter T was transmitted twice at a very loud volume on the merchant vessel short-wave frequency, 36m, at 1020, and three Ts with a very long dash for each character were sent between 1034 and 1036.' The steamer was ordered to stop and *Leipzig* lowered a boat to investigate. The vessel was the Danish *Charkov*, wearing neutrality markings and appearing on the German Free List. Upon receiving this information, Lütjens gave orders that the steamer was not to be searched. At 1110 the German cruisers left the *Charkov* and resumed their triangular formation at high speed.

At 1115 an unidentified aircraft was sighted in the clouds by *Köln*. At the second sighting the aircraft signalled the word 'Max' by hand-lamp. This was not the German recognition signal of the day, which was 'U'. The aircraft was identified as a Lockheed, keeping out of flak range. A few minutes later two low-flying aircraft approached the cruisers. These were two Heinkel 115 floatplanes, which fired two red stars, the correct signal. This must have been seen by the Lockheed, for in the later air attack the British aircraft fired off red stars for the benefit of *Nürnberg*.

At 1118 *Köln* noted that the code 'TT' was sent twice on the 36m shipping wavelength and observed, 'From our wireless location monitoring, this is the steamer *Charkov* warning of her own presence in the vicinity or is for the benefit of the enemy signals centre. As the transmission is being made on short-wave, direct co-operation with submarines and aircraft is improbable.'

At 1120 the position of the five approaching destroyers was reported by the two German He 115 aircraft to be about 40 miles west-south-west of the cruisers. Lütjens ordered the three cruisers to steer 240° to meet the destroyers.

The scene was now set for the disaster at 1125. At that moment, *Leipzig*'s lookout reported sighting two vessels on the horizon where the German destroyers were expected to appear, and the two Heinkel 115 floatplanes arrived over the cruisers to replace the shipboard aircraft sent off to Sylt. The senior observer of the latter reported:

On nearing the cruisers on a north-west course, I commenced the exchange of recognition signals, 'U'. After I had given 'U' twice we turned off a little to starboard in order not to overfly the cruisers directly while awaiting a definite response in recognition. As we did so, we all saw the tracks of a fan of about five torpedoes heading for *Leipzig*. Aligning my aircraft along the course of the torpedoes, I gave a U-boat warning at once—the Morse character 'U' repeated several times.

A few seconds later a torpedo struck *Leipzig* amidships on the port side with a loud explosion and a great column of water rose up, followed by a large developing cloud of smoke. The observer's report continued: 'Above the spot from where the submarine had fired we dropped two SC 250s, which failed to explode although our height and attitude were correct. After that we saw the submarine showing his periscope and heading north-east and gunned it.'

In Lütjens' report the senior aircraft observer was sharply criticised. The use of the Morse character 'U' to warn a surface warship of a submarine is not German naval procedure. The textbook instruction was to fire white stars and indicate the submarine's position by dropping a buoy and flying tight circles over the location. The Morse signal 'U' was the aircraft recognition signal of the day and would therefore not have been interpreted by the cruiser's officers as a submarine warning.

Aboard *Leipzig* the track of an approaching torpedo was seen 500m off, and this was too late to avoid impact. The order 'Hard to port' had just been put into effect when the torpedo hit amidships.

Aboard *Nürnberg* and *Köln*, 1,200m distant, there was an immediate suspicion that *Leipzig* had incorrectly identified enemy aircraft as friendly, for from *Nürnberg* the aircraft seemed to be in a classic attack position and *Köln* also recorded that it had at first been assumed to be an aerial torpedo attack. At the order 'Signal Green 9' *Nürnberg* and *Köln* executed a turn-away at high speed, but as the turn was still completing two torpedoes were seen approaching *Nürnberg* on the starboard quarter running parallel and 15–20 m apart. The helm was put hard to port, but the cruiser responded only slowly because she still had way on to starboard, and one of the torpedoes struck the starboard side well forward alongside compartments XIV/XV.

Calculations showed that *Leipzig* and *Nürnberg* received one torpedo each from a fan of three, the third having missed *Nürnberg*. Four to five minutes after *Nürnberg* was hit, three more torpedo tracks were sighted astern of the cruiser. These exploded harmlessly on the sea bed, one about 500m astern, and two about the same distance away to port. Shortly afterwards *Nürnberg* sighted a partially surfaced submarine directly astern about 5km off. 'C' turret opened fire, causing the submarine to dive after about 20 seconds. The wireless monitoring section reported that the submarine was *Salmon*, with six bow torpedo tubes. Following the hit, *Nürnberg* reduced speed to about 12kt, later increasing to 18. Her flak fire control was out of commission but her seaworthiness was not affected.

Aboard the approaching German destroyers the detonations and smoke had been observed aboard *Hermann Künne* and *Friedrich Ihn*. The bearing was so far off the rendezvous point, however, that the destroyer leader decided that the activity did not involve the cruisers and must be between aircraft and a submarine. For this reason the destroyers elected not to approach the site of the activity.

Between 1130 and 1210 *Nürnberg* and *Köln* followed an escape pattern which involved proceeding clockwise in a square, followed by a south-easterly heading on exit-

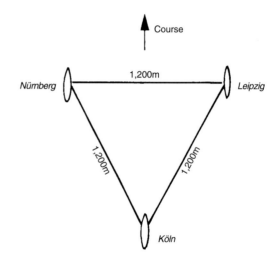

Above: Sailing formation at commencement of operation, 12 December 1939 (per BdA report).

ing. *Leipzig* was out of sight but also heading south-east, making 12kt on her cruise diesel, all her boiler furnaces having been extinguished.

The five destroyers were required urgently to give anti-submarine protection to the damaged cruisers but had not materialised contrary to expectations. A signal, '1126, *Nürnberg* and *Leipzig* torpedoed Grid Square 3747. BdA.', had not been transmitted because of a defective aerial and simultaneous telegraphist error, and as the destroyer leader (FdZ) had not received this signal (since he had not tuned in on the long-wave close zone in accordance with standing instructions), at 1137 *Vizeadmiral* Lütjens requested the rendezvous through the Fleet short-wave band. For the critical ten-minute period after the attack, complete confusion had reigned ashore, but even now the destroyers remained unaware of what was amiss.

Between 1212 and 1222 three Hampden bombers—probably those beaten off ninety minutes or so earlier by *Bruno Heinemann*—attacked *Nürnberg*. The first bomb run resulted in flak damage to the attacker and was not pressed home. One of the two He 115 escort aircraft reported:

> *Nürnberg* was shooting with all her flak batteries. I had received the order from *Köln* 'Stay with *Nürnberg*.' I flew close escort to *Nürnberg*. This was at quite low altitude because a Lockheed bomber occasionally came out of the clouds and the cruiser then fired at it above me. I received a Morse message from *Nürnberg*: 'Request battle group to drive off that contact keeper.' Shortly afterwards, two 50kg bombs fell astern of the cruiser's starboard side. After that, the contact aircraft disappeared.

This was the second bomb run. One bomb fell about 40m directly astern, the other 20m off, abeam the after turret. On the third run both bombs fell about 800m astern of *Nürnberg* and exploded after a delay. Skilful manoeuvring by *Kapitän zur See* Klüber and a very heavy flak defence ensured that *Nürnberg* escaped damage. The aircraft made off at 1246. The other two cruisers were not attacked.

More than an hour after *Nürnberg* and *Leipzig* had been torpedoed, the destroyers had still not effected the rendezvous, and as it seemed to Lütjens that a navigational problem must exist he decided to wireless the FdZ his position, course and speed and a homing signal as from 1245 and sent off the aircraft circling *Leipzig* to scout for the destroyers. The aircraft failed to establish contact because of poor visibility.

At 1250 the FdZ detached *Friedrich Ihn* (boiler trouble) and *Erich Steinbrinck* (water in fuel oil) while he proceeded with *Hermann Künne*, *Bruno Heinemann* and *Richard Beitzen* to the original rendezvous position. A few moments later his telegraphists intercepted a message from an aircraft with the call-sign 'S4EH' reporting damage to a light cruiser. This was the first he knew of the incident, and he decided not to recall the two detached destroyers since his force of three would be sufficient to cover one damaged light cruiser.

Lütjens had repeated his 1245 signal at 1250 and 1303, at which time *Nürnberg* and *Köln* sighted *Leipzig* and closed to within two nautical miles to exchange information by Morse lamp, *Köln* being given the job of providing *Leipzig* with flak cover. At 1340 the three German destroyers were seen steaming up; *Richard Beitzen* and *Bruno Heinemann* took up station on *Leipzig* while *Nürnberg* received the protection of *Hermann Künne* with *Köln* off the port quarter. Three low-flying aircraft aircraft circled the group. As it was considered possible that enemy submarines or destroyers might infiltrate the German Bight behind the mine barrier for a night attack, strict radio silence was imposed.

Nürnberg could make 15kt and reach coastal waters by nightfall and thus was sent on with only *Hermann Künne* for escort, the two ships steering 135° homing in on the Hornum coastal beacon. Her casualties were fifteen slightly wounded from the torpedo hit.

In his report of 6 February 1940 *Admiral* Saalwächter, CinC Naval Group West, criticised Lütjens for (a) stopping to investigate the steamer *Charkov*, which may have given the British submarine commander the opportunity to line up his torpedo attack; (b) his poor handling of the aerial forces generally; and (c) exposing the undamaged cruiser *Köln* to danger by not detaching her once sufficient escort forces had assembled to see home the damaged *Leipzig*. Air Commander West was advised regarding the use of unauthorised methods of warning of submarine attack.

In matters directly pertaining to *Nürnberg* in his report on the mission cited earlier, *Admiral* Marschall condemned the triangular sailing formation as being more favourable for submarine attack than close formation, especially where escort forces were absent. He criticised Lütjens for stopping to investigate the *Charkov* when Lütjens had made it clear that the monitoring of commerce was excluded on this operation.

Marschall remarked that two aircraft flying anti-submarine patrol for three cruisers was a very moderate escort. He sympathised with the fliers with regard to the most unfortunate coincidence that the Morse letter of im-

Below: Battle sketch, BdA, 13 December 1939 (from Appendix 4, BdA Report).

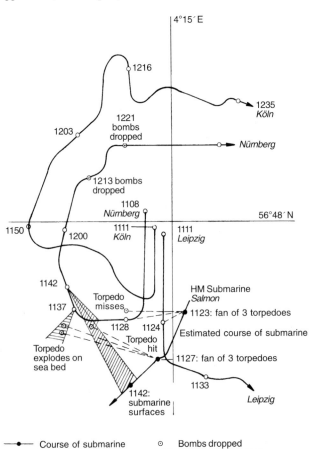

provised warning, 'U' for 'Unterseeboot', was the same letter of the day as for aircraft recognition purposes. The aircraft had seen the torpedoes heading for *Leipzig* and was supposed to give warning by firing off white stars, circling the spot and attempting to bomb the submarine all at the same time. Air Commander West would be advised accordingly. *Nürnberg* and the FdZ were responsible for the error in signals procedures.*

The shipyard repairs to *Nürnberg* kept her out of the Norwegian campaign in April. During this period two sets of torpedo tubes aft were unshipped and a degaussing system was fitted. On 18 April *Konteradmiral* Schmundt was appointed acting BdA and raised his pennant aboard *Nürnberg* in the shipyard, remaining aboard until 3 June. After release and working up her engines, the cruiser rejoined the BdA squadron and, escorted by the torpedo-boats *Jaguar* and *Falke*, proceeded to Trondheim, where *Konteradmiral* Schmundt disembarked. Between 14 and 19 June, in an operation codenamed 'Nora', *Nürnberg*, the destroyer *Erich Steinbrinck* and the 2nd Minesweeping Flotilla escorted the troopship *Levante* transporting the 3rd Mountain Division from Trondheim to Elvegardsmoen and returning with the paratroop force relieved there. On 25 July *Nürnberg* and the destroyers *Hans Lody*, *Friedrich Ihn*, *Paul Jacobi* and *Karl Galster* sailed from Trondheim for Kiel as escort for the damaged battleship *Gneisenau*. On 26 July they were joined by the torpedo-boats *Luchs*, *Kondor*, *Jaguar* and *Iltis*, and the same day *Luchs* was torpedoed and sunk by the British submarine *Swordfish* with the loss of 89 lives.

On 1 August the post of BdA was redesignated BdK (*Befehlshaber der Kreuzer*, CinC Cruisers). *Nürnberg* remained flagship of a squadron which consisted of the heavy cruisers *Prinz Eugen*, *Admiral Hipper*, *Admiral Scheer*, *Lützow* (ex *Deutschland*), the light cruisers *Köln* and *Emden* and the Fleet tender *Gazelle*. *Kapitän zur See* Leo Kreisch became the *Nürnberg*'s sixth commander in August. No further operations were found for the cruiser, which, with other large naval units, remained on standby should Operation 'Seelöwe', the invasion of Britain, proceed. On 4 December Operation 'Frankfurt', a planned minelaying sortie for *Nürnberg*, *Köln* and six torpedo-boats in the Kattegat and Skagerrak, was cancelled because of unfavourable weather.

Early in 1941 OKM issued an instruction reclassifying the four surviving light cruisers, *Nürnberg*, *Köln*, *Leipzig* and *Emden*, as training ships 'with no further operational deployment as from 7 February 1941', and aboard *Nürnberg* the BdK hauled down his command flag on 18 Febru-

ary. *Kapitän zur See* Ernst von Studnitz became the seventh commander of the cruiser in March. During the year the 6m rangefinder was replaced temporarily by an FuMO 21 radar mattress.

Following the opening of the campaign against the Soviet Union on 22 June 1941 the cruiser was recalled to operations to form part of the Baltic Fleet. On 23 September the battleship *Tirpitz*, the heavy cruiser *Admiral Scheer*, *Nürnberg*, *Köln* and destroyers left Swinemünde for the Gulf of Finland to intercept Russian warships if they attempted to intern in Sweden. *Admiral Scheer* was damaged by a depth-charge explosion on deck on 25 September and dropped out. On the 27th the remainder of the group, accompanied by a large force of minesweepers and small craft, appeared off the Abo-Aland skerries, but the Red Flag Fleet had no intention of leaving Kronstadt and when the operation was called off in October *Nürnberg* reverted to her role as a training cruiser.

From the beginning of 1942 the aircraft and catapult installation was discarded and the FuMO 21 aerial on the bridge was replaced by an FuMO 25 on a battlemast mounting. The cruiser was used mainly as a training ship until November, when she was called upon to replace *Admiral Scheer*, which was returning home from Norway for an urgent refit. *Nürnberg* arrived at Narvik on 2 December and subsequently shifted round the various anchorages, but was otherwise not used.

In 1943 *Nürnberg* was included in the general decommissioning of all heavy naval units and returned to Germany in May to resume her role as a training ship in the Baltic. *Kapitän zur See* Gerhardt Böhmig became her eighth commander in June.

During 1944 an FuMO 63 *Hohentwiel* aerial was mounted on the after pole mast. *Nürnberg* continued as a training ship until the autumn, when any vessel afloat which was to any extent operational became needed urgently. Initial duties were convoy and escort tasks until the situation became disastrous a few weeks later. In October 1944 *Kapitän zur See* Helmuth Giessler became *Nürnberg*'s ninth and final commander.

On 3 January 1945 *Nürnberg* and the minelayers *Linz* and *Elsass* left Swinemünde to set a field off the southern tip of Norway. On the 5th, while laying, *Elsass* was lost with 87 hands after striking one of her own mines. On the 13th and 14th the 'Titus' minefield was laid in the Skagerrak, after which *Nürnberg* escorted various refugee transports

---

* For further details from official reports regarding this mission see under *Leipzig*.—G.B.

through the mine-free channel. On 24 January *Nürnberg* was in Oslo Fjord with the minelayers *Linz* and *Lothringen*, and on the 27th she reached Copenhagen, where she remained until the capitulation since no fuel was available.

Following the surrender to British forces in northern Germany on 5 May, Danish resistance fighters attempted to seize the cruiser, and both sides suffered losses in a violent quayside shoot-out. On 6 May the first British naval vessels arrived, but the British did not take charge of the German warships and crews until the 22nd of the month, when orders were received for them to be brought from Copenhagen to Wilhelmshaven.

On 24 May a convoy consisting of the heavy cruiser HMS *Devonshire*, *Prinz Eugen* and *Nürnberg*, the light cruiser HMS *Dido* and the destroyers HMS *Quiberon* and *Savage* left Copenhagen, the two British heavy units departing from the convoy on the 25th with a signal to the senior German officer 'Auf Wiedersehen until better times.' Two minesweepers replaced the British cruisers. On 26 May *Nürnberg* entered Wilhelmshaven through Entrance III and made fast at the Seydlitzbrücke alongside the accommodation ship *Monte Pascoal*.

Under the terms of the Potsdam Agreement the victorious powers had agreed that the German Fleet was to be shared amongst themselves by 15 February 1946. At the end of Novemver 1945 the British Admiralty had received information pointing to the possibility that the Germans were planning a large-scale sabotage, particularly against those units assigned to the Soviets, either at Christmas or in any case before the ships were at readiness on 5 January 1946. Accordingly, arrangements were made to

'pounce' on the ships without prior notice on some day after 18 December 1945, and this took the Germans by surprise. On 2 January *Nürnberg*, wearing the flag of Soviet Vice-Admiral Rall and the Soviet naval ensign, set off from Wilhelmshaven for Libau via Kiel. When in the lock chamber with the target ship *Hessen*, the seaward gate of the Raeder Lock refused to open. The personal efforts of *Konteradmiral* Kurt Weyher and suggestions from many other people were unsuccessful in clearing the jam, and *Nürnberg* and *Hessen* had to be moved by tugs to the Tirpitz Locks and taken through as soon as some smaller ships had left. Apart from this incident—a subtle piece of sabotage 'done so cleverly that nothing could be proved'—there were no other last-minute defects and 'the whole party eventually steamed away in tolerably good order', according to Rear Admiral Hutton in his report to the British Naval CinC Germany.

The German ships were escorted by HMS *Hambledon* to Brunsbüttel and then by HMS *Holderness* as far as Russian territorial waters at 55° 07´ N 13° 13´ E, where Russian escorts took over. At Libau the German crew left *Nürnberg* and returned to Wilhelmshaven aboard the depot ship Otto Wünsche.

Nürnberg was commissioned into the Soviet Navy as *Admiral Makarov* and was used mainly as a training ship. The torpedo tubes, light flak and searchlight platforms around the funnel were removed and Russian electronic equipment was installed, but otherwise her outward appearance hardly changed during her service. She was decommissioned in 1960 and scrapped.

Opposite page: The World War I light cruiser *Nürnberg*, 3,469 tons, was launched at the Kaiserliche Werft, Kiel, on 28 August 1906 and commissioned on 10 April 1908. At the outbreak of war in August 1914 *Nürnberg* (*Fregattenkapitän* von Schönberg) formed part of *Vizeadmiral* von Spee's East Asia Cruiser Squadron. On 8 September, in company with the tender *Titania*, the cruiser was detached to destroy the wireless station and transpacific cable on Fanning Island near Christmas Island. At the Battle of Coronel on 1 November 1914 *Nürnberg* arrived on the scene late but finished off the crippled armoured cruiser *Monmouth*. On 8 December 1914 the Cruiser Squadron approached the Falkland Islands intending to invade; from the islands armed occupation troops were seen lining the decks of *Gneisenau* and *Nürnberg*. Unknown to von Spee, a vastly superior British squadron consisting of the battlecruisers *Invincible* and *Indefatigable* and four smaller cruisers were anchored at Port Stanley. Von Spee fled and the British force put to sea in pursuit. As soon as the two battlecruisers began to endanger his light cruisers during the chase, von Spee decided to take on the heavy units with *Scharnhorst* and *Gneisenau*, so allowing the three smaller ships to escape independently if they could. *Nürnberg* was pursued and engaged by the 9,800-ton armoured cruiser *Kent*. The German ship was in poor condition mechanically and could make no more than 22kt. Her lightweight 10.5cm guns were no match for *Kent*. The two ships fought for about two hours. At 1826 *Nürnberg* was out of ammunition and almost adrift, but the ensign was not lowered until 1857. She sank at 1937, and in the heavy seas there was little hope of rescuing many of her crew; in the end, the British picked up twelve, of whom five later died aboard *Kent*. *Kent* herself lost eight dead. Armament: 10 × 10.5cm and eight 5.2cm guns, two torpedo tubes. Dimensions: 116.8 × 13.3 × 5.24m. Machinery: triple-expansion steam engines driven by eleven coal-fired watertube boilers, speed 23.4kt. Final complement including reservists: about 360. The photograph shows *Nürnberg* in light grey livery before her departure for East Asia.

Right, upper: The light cruiser *Nürnberg* (ii), 5,440 tons, was launched at Howaldtswerke, Kiel, on 4 April 1916 and commissioned on 15 February 1917. She was interned at Scapa Flow in 1918 and, having survived the attempt of her crew to scuttle the ship on 21 June 1919, was expended by the Royal Navy as a target ship on 7 July 1922. Armament: 8 × 15cm guns, 2 × 8.8cm flak, four torpedo tubes. Machinery: steam turbines driven by eight coal-fired and six oil-fired boilers, speed 27.5kt. Dimensions: 145.8 × 14.2 × 5.96m. In the photograph the ship is seen leaving Grand Harbour at Wilhelmshaven bound for Scapa Flow on 17 November 1918.

Right, lower: The first hull frames of the new cruiser, *Nürnberg* (iii).

Left, top: The launching ceremony viewed from a slipway crane. To the right is the honour guard, behind which a vast throng of spectators has gathered.
Left, centre: *Nürnberg* enters the waters of the basin.
Left, bottom: Taken in tow by tugs, the hull is steered towards the quayside.

Right: *Nürnberg* in an advanced stage of fitting-out, her 15cm turrets, battlemast, funnel and searchlight platforms mounted. Notice the light anti-torpedo bulge at the waterline. The ship is unladen and rides high in the water.

Below: A port-side view of the cruiser fitting out.

Bottom: *Nürnberg* completed and ready to enter service.

Left, upper and lower: On 2 November 1935 the naval ensign and commander's pennant were hoisted, signalling that *Nürnberg* was in commission. The ensign was replaced a few days later throughout the Fleet by the *Reich* War Flag.
Above and below: *Nürnberg* seen from ahead on either bow while leaving Kiel. She has already been fitted with a pole mast and crosstrees abaft the funnel, and the shipboard aircraft equipment and Heinkel 60 floatplane. The anti-torpedo blister is clearly visible on the waterline. In the lower photograph the cruiser, as flagship of the BdA, wears the appropriate command flag at the foretop.

Above: *Nürnberg* at Kiel with lively traffic at the jack ladder amidships. The port mooring boom is extended. Crew members work on the port anchor.

Left: Large German KdF ('Strength Through Joy') passenger ships were often fitted into naval exercises. Here *Nürnberg*'s crew parade the upper deck while passing one of these liners.

Right, upper: The light cruisers *Nürnberg*, *Leipzig* and one of the 'K' class in starboard echelon formation, seen from the quarterdeck of the pocket-battleship *Deutschland* during a naval exercise.

Right, lower: *Nürnberg* (right) in Spanish waters in 1936, seen from the stern of a torpedo-boat. The ship at left is the French destroyer *Tartu*.

Below: A broadside view of the cruiser. The *Reich* War Flag is set at the foretop.

Left, top: *Nürnberg* with the torpedo-boat *Tiger* alongside.

Left, centre: A midships view showing the Heinkel 60 floatplane with national markings. Alongside is a fleet tanker.

Left, bottom: *Nürnberg* with the passenger liner *Der Deutsche* abeam.

Right, upper: *Nürnberg* during naval exercises in 1938. Notice the minelaying rails overhanging the stern.

Right, lower: *Nürnberg* approaching Hamburg for the launch of the battleship *Bismarck*, February 1939, her ship's company parading the upper deck. Notice the rather high bridge with its 6m rangefinder—a compromise solution because of the poor view afforded by having the battlemast and command centre set further aft than aboard *Leipzig*.

Below left: 'B' and 'C' turrets traversed to port. Projecting above 'B' turret are the twin exhausts of the cruise diesel; in contrast to the 'K' class's demountable pipes, aboard *Leipzig* and *Nürnberg* they were fixed.

Below right: Gunnery practice: 'B' and 'C' turrets firing abaft the port beam.

 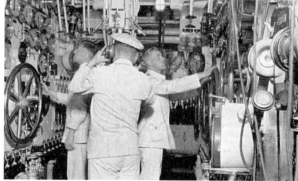

Top, left and right: The engine room.
Above, left and right: Ships of this size were fitted with fully equipped workshops so that even complicated repairs could be carried out aboard. These two photographs show the engine room workshop.

Below: *Nürnberg* in Norwegian waters in June 1940 with an Arado 196 floatplane, the now-standard issue for larger German warships. During this period the aircraft flew covering patrols for Army units ashore.

Above: Another view of the ship in Norwegian waters.
Below: In autumn 1941 *Nürnberg* was attached to the Baltic Fleet. This photograph, taken from a destroyer, shows the cruiser (right) being followed by destroyers *Z 26* and *Z 27*.

Left, upper: A photograph taken from *Tirpitz* during the same period as the previous illustration shows *Nürnberg* and *Köln* about to cross the battleships's wake.

Left, lower, and this page: *Nürnberg* at Swinemünde in 1941, showing the Baltic camouflage pattern from three different perspectives.

Above: This photograph of *Nürnberg*, starboard side, demonstrates how disruptive camouflage breaks up the ship's contours. Notice the radar antenna just below the foretop.

Left, upper: *Nürnberg* at Flensburg in 1942. A smokescreen is being laid over the harbour following an air raid alarm.

Left, lower: *Nürnberg* seen from astern at Flensburg, 1942. The additional liferafts secured to the turret side (left), the cruise diesel exhausts behind 'B' turret and the catapult installation are clearly visible.

Right, upper: In 1942 *Nürnberg* was transferred to Norway, where she is seen here inside her net defences. In the background is the heavy cruiser *Admiral Hipper*.

Right, lower: *Nürnberg* wearing typical camouflage for Norwegian operations. Notice the additional radar antennas mounted on the battlemast and the antennas of the rangefinding radar at the foretop.

Above: The midships section of *Nürnberg*, port side, 1942.
Below left: Looking over the bow from the bridge. Notice the platform with an additional 2cm quadruple flak.
Below right: 'B' turret in 1942. The shielding on the turret roof is for the additional 2cm flak mounted there.

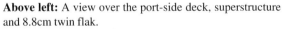

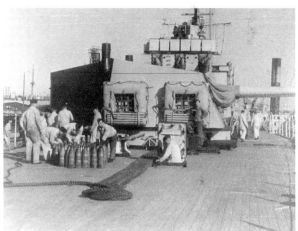

Above left: A view over the port-side deck, superstructure and 8.8cm twin flak.

Above right: The bridge and battlemast. On the latter is the radar mattress, at the foretop the aerials for the rangefinding radar.

Below left: Signallers on 'A' turret roof, bridge projection and bridge proper under semaphore instruction. Notice the radar mattress.

Below right: Looking forward from the quarterdeck. 'C' turret, with square Marx liferafts secured to the turret wall, has been turned to starboard in order to embark ammunition.

Left, upper: In addition to the radar antennas on the battlemast and at the foretop, *Nürnberg* now carries a *Hohentwiel* aerial on the aft pole mast. The after torpedo-tube mounting has been left ashore.

Left, lower: An Allied photograph taken on 26 July 1943 showing *Nürnberg* within a barrier of nets at Swinemünde. To the right is a freighter, in the basin numerous lighters.

Above: *Nürnberg* after the capitulation, alongside a Copenhagen quayside and protected against attack by barbed-wire barriers.

Right lower: Bringing ammunition ashore in Copenhagen.

Above: Assembling for delivery to Wilhelmshaven: a view from the heavy cruiser *Prinz Eugen* to *Nürnberg* (right) and the British light cruiser *Dido* (left).

Below: During the voyage to Wilhelmshaven two Liberator bombers of Coastal Command pass overhead.

Right, upper: Entering a lock chamber at Wilhelmshaven by way of Entrance III. At left is one of the British escort destroyers.

Right, lower: *Nürnberg* at the Bonte Quay, Wilhelmshaven. Notice the anti-mine degaussing coil along the ship's side.

Left, upper: *Nürnberg* at the Bonte Quay with the destroyer
Z 6 (*Theodor Riedel*) alongside.

Left, lower: *Nürnberg* on morning of 2 January 1946 as the
Soviet-crewed cruiser heads for the lock on the first stage of
her voyage to Libau.

Above and right: The cruiser entered Entrance IV (Raeder
Lock) in company with the target ship *Hessen* (an old
Imperial battleship). A delay occurred when the lock gate to
seaward could not be opened. These two photographs show
the cruiser in the lock chamber.

Above and below: Because of the defect, which was caused by sabotage, the two ships had to leave Entrance IV and proceed instead by way of Entrance III (Tirpitz Lock), one to each lock chamber under tug assistance. D 4 is *Wapel* and D 35 *Wachtel*.

Right, upper and lower: Tirpitz Lock opens and both *Nürnberg*, under her own steam and flying the pennant of Vice-Admiral Rall, Soviet Navy, and *Hessen*, under tow, reach tidal water. Rall was German-born and had served as an officer in the Imperial German Navy in the First World War.

Above and below: *Nürnberg* heads for the Schillig Roads on her voyage of no return to the Soviet Union.

Conclusions

As the first new cruiser of the postwar *Reichsmarine*, *Emden* was designed and built to modified plans for the *Cöln* class cruisers of the defunct Imperial Navy. Manufacturing capacity in Germany immediately after the war was so desperate that it was planned to equip the new hull with second-hand boilers and engines from the scrapyard, but these and similar ideas were prohibited by the Allied Naval Control Commission (NIACC). The completed *Emden* complied strictly with the limitations of the Versailles Treaty. She was the only partially coal-fired German unit above torpedo-boat size built after World War I and was designed for use primarily as a training cruiser.

The five later German light cruisers were 'children of their time'—the result of what designers had found possible to engineer within the limitations of the Washington Agreement and a vast improvement on *Emden* except as regards seaworthiness. There were minor infringements of the limitations, unintentional or otherwise, but if these were identified by the control organs and NIACC they were tolerated. The great weakness of the 'K' cruisers—*Königsberg*, *Köln* and *Karlsruhe*—was their light construction. The fault lay not with the designers but in the restrictions of the Versailles Treaty.

The military requirement was for big hitting power, an ability to take punishment, great range and long endurance at sea; a compromise had to be made somewhere, and accordingly the ships lacked steadfastness. In difficult sea conditions the weaknesses showed. On a number of occasions, *Köln*'s superstructure had to be reinforced: the failure of welded seams at joints and corners, especially around the funnels and on the upper deck, also occurred on her sister-ships. Early on, speed restrictions were imposed in bad weather, while in really severe weather the ships had to find shelter. Their large length-to-beam ratio meant that they rolled immoderately and ran the risk of capsize in extremely heavy conditions. In the spring of 1936 *Karlsruhe* barely survived this fate when she encountered a hurricane in the Pacific and threatened to break in two. She had to be bolted over at San Diego to keep her in one piece for the transatlantic crossing home. As a result of these weaknesses, the three 'K' class cruisers were confined to the North Sea and Baltic. *Leipzig* and *Nürnberg* were equally suspect.

Of the six ships, only *Emden* was oceanworthy: eventually the others were only allowed to stray beyond home waters (e.g. to Spain) subject to restrictions, and essentially their operations were limited to fine-weather periods. At all times the forward and after fuel bunkers had to be emptied first, and their fuel was so important for stability that the amount aboard was not permitted to fall below 680m³ (150m³ in Nürnberg). This meant over-firequent refuelling, which ruled out operations beyond coastal waters in wartime. Thus the ships were useless as commerce raiders.

When designing warships naval architects set aside an allowance known as the 'Admiralty Reserve' for weight increases caused by later modifications. This was not available on the five later light cruisers since the architects had built right up to the 6,000-ton displacement limit. Additions such as the aircraft catapult, new fire control systems and new weapons increased the topside weight of individual ships. At commissioning *Königsberg* was 354 tonnes in excess, *Karlsruhe* 247 tonnes, *Köln* 277 tonnes and *Leipzig* 382 tonnes. Without question, this affected their stability and was the reason why the 'K' cruisers had to unship their catapults.

The three 'K' class cruisers were expected to remain in service until 1947–48 and major refits were scheduled to improve stability and seakeeping. *Karlsruhe* was the first and only unit to enter the yard, excess demand and the outbreak of war putting an end to major conversion plans for the other four cruisers. She was fitted with a second outer shell stretching from keel to upper deck about 70cm outside the original side. The new plating was a very strong material of armour quality. Side bulges would have increased metacentric height to reduce rolling and make the ship a more stable gun platform in exchange for settling deeper in the case of flooding, but the architects decided against it.

The engine rooms of the latter five ships were generally uncomplicated, reliable to operate and modern in their arrangement. All five ships had steam turbines with a cruising diesel. In the 'K' class cruisers the two shafts were driven by either turbine or diesel but not both together; in *Leipzig* and *Nürnberg* the diesel had a separate central shaft. In either case, however, the ship had to stop and drift while any changeover was made. In wartime this could be fatal, as was demonstrated by the collision between *Leipzig* and *Prinz Eugen* during a coupling changeover off Gotenhafen in 1944.*

The Versailles Treaty forced German designers to spread the engine room space over a greater area than was normal. Of the sixteen compartments, the ship's machinery occupied half in the 'K' class cruisers

The light cruisers were never able to meet the modest demands made of them. At the outbreak of war *Emden* and the three 'K' class ships were already practically worn out, *Leipzig* was past her best and *Nürnberg* was only operational within limits. September 1939 found the German Navy unprepared, in upheaval and half-way through a phase of reconstruction. The Commander-in-Chief, *Admiral* Raeder, had piloted naval thinking since 1928 and stamped his authority in such a manner that one can al-

most talk of a 'Raeder Era' as one does of a 'Tirpitz Era'. Raeder did not lead from the front but had comprehensive staff and administrative experience. He was convinced that in war the Navy's priority was to guarantee the flow of imports of raw materials into Germany. Commerce warfare was secondary to this. The Great War had demonstrated the extent to which German cruisers operating beyond European waters depended on supply. Coaling stations had been carefully set up before the war, but British capital and influence convinced most neutrals to adopt a stricter interpretation of neutrality as regards German colliers than anticipated. All German cruisers at large were eventually tracked down and sunk or fell victim to misfortune. The merchant raiders—heavily armed steamers masquerading under innocent disguises—were more successful for a while, but the widespread introduction of wireless telegraphy made their job increasingly difficult. Nearer to home it was left to the U-boats to attempt to achieve victory by blockading Great Britain, but unrestricted submarine warfare was hampered by having too few boats for the task.†

---

* As the various reports quoted herein show, the collision occurred as a result of *Leipzig* proceeding in the wrong lane of the swept channel several minutes after the changeover. Nevertheless, being adrift for ten minutes while the changeover was made, in an area where an enemy submarine alert was in force, must have contributed to the commander's error.—G.B.

† The author made the point in his *Pocket Battleships of the Deutschland Class* of this series that warfare against merchant shipping on the high seas is the business of light cruisers, and what he said bears repetition here. The Royal and US Navies had themselves found an 8in armament too ponderous for the task. For commerce raiding beyond coastal waters, all six German light cruisers were completely unsuitable. With the exception of the pocket-battleships, German heavy units did not have sufficient radius of action for effective operations and relied on frequent refuelling. *Admiral Scheer* proved what could be achieved far from home with adroit handling and a well-organised system of supply. Instead of the heavy and light cruisers with which it equipped itself, the German Navy might have been better served by a class of well-armoured, fast, diesel-driven light cruisers for commerce raiding. Consideration was only given to the question too late. In November 1933 *Admiral* Raeder had decided in favour of the high-pressure steam turbine for warships. Years of polemic ensued, and not until 1938 did the subject of steam turbine or diesel become topical again, when the majority was now in favour of diesel. But years which could have been devoted to the development of an improved diesel were lost. MAN-Diesel had continued the work privately, but they lacked the active support of the *Kriegsmarine*, which had given the nod to

steam. Thus in 1938 the German Navy made a belated return to designing diesel-driven warships, but after the outbreak of war planning was suspended except for an experimental destroyer, for which contracts were placed with Deschimag Bremen on 25 November 1942 under Yard Number 1109, with three others to follow.

The prototype, described more fully in the author's *Die Deutschen Zerstörer* of this series, was *Z 51* of Type 1942 (2,720 tons operational displacement; dimensions 114.3 × 11 × 4.3m maximum; main armament 4 × 12.7cm guns in single gunhouses two fore and two aft, 20 flak, eight torpedo tubes; six MAN V12Z 32/44 double-acting two-stroke diesels each of 12,600 hp;, three shafts; top speed 36kt; bunkers 553 tonnes; complement 247 officers and men). The dimensions and main armament were similar to those of the pre-World War I small cruisers. Undoubtedly this development was a great step for the Navy and the design was evidence of marked 'oceanic' thinking initiated by the lack of pure cruisers. With its diesels this destroyer/cruiser would have had a great range analogous to that of the *Deutschland* class pocket-battleships and Type IX U-boats. But by then it was too late.—G.B.

Index of Ships